JAMAICAN RECORDINGS
A HISTORY OF THE JAMAICAN RECORDING INDUSTRY

THE BIRTH OF SKA
FROM MENTO TO STUDIO ONE
Noel Hawks & Jah Floyd

PUBLISHED BY
JAMAICAN RECORDINGS PUBLISHING

All rights reserved. No part of this book may be used or reproduced in any manner whatsoever, including information storage or retrieval systems, without written permission except in the case of brief quotations embodied in critical articles and reviews.
For information: Jamaican Recordings
First published in Great Britain in 2021 by Jamaican Recordings Publishing
Copyright Jamaican Recordings Publishing 2021
Photographs Copyright as credited
Designed by Gary Hall
ISBN 978-0-9569991-1-5
www.jamaicanrecordings.com
℗JAMAICAN RECORDINGS 2021 ©JAMAICAN RECORDINGS 2021

CONTENTS

Introduction

Chapter 1 — Page 15
How It All Began
Motta's Recording Studio

Chapter 2 — Page 31
Mento Gets Another Mention
Chin's Radio Services
& The Caribbean Recording Company Ltd

Chapter 3 — Page 45
Sound Systems Were Like Our Radio Station
RJR & JBC

Chapter 4 — Page 81
Federal Country... Another Hit!
Records Ltd & Federal Records

Chapter 5 — Page 125
Dancing To The Music Of Sir Coxsone The Downbeat
Studio One

Every effort has been made to obtain the necessary permissions with reference to copyright material both illustrative and quoted. We apologise for any omissions in this respect and will be pleased to make the appropriate acknowledgments in any future editions

King St., Kingston, Jamaica, B.W.I.

KING STREET, KINGSTON, JAMAICA

Introduction

"The glamour boys in the show business world may be the vocalists, musicians, dancers and other entertainers who are always on show for the public, but behind the scenes are a group of individuals without whose foresight, planning and drive these artistes would never tick. These behind the scenes operators are invariably denied any kudos associated with a successful promotion or presentation, yet they continue to make a substantial contribution to show business in this island."

'Greatest Jamaican Beat'

The importance of recorded music to the history of reggae can never, ever be overstated. These are the stories of the men and women who made the records, made the music available worldwide and how they achieved this. It aims to be a 'popular history' of the studios, manufacturers, musicians, arrangers and record producers and the story of the birth and growth of the Jamaican recording industry told through firsthand accounts wherever possible. We felt that these stories were sufficiently important to use as the basis for a collection of recollections. Sadly, a number of the luminaries we have had the pleasure to interview are now no longer with us; the majority of the interviews featured here were conducted over the last two decades for a number of different projects. They were originally used for the liner notes of re-releases and re-issues for a variety of record labels including Black Solidarity, Blood & Fire, Dub Store Records, Greensleeves, Jamaican Recordings, Kingston Sounds, Patate Records, Pressure Sounds, Soul Jazz, Trojan, Universal and VP.

Each chapter is a self contained story of a particular studio so that, although the chapters are intended to follow chronologically, the narrative often gets ahead of the stories detailed in the subsequent chapters. All of the stories are varied and, although not all of Kingston's studios had that legendary atmosphere, we have tried to include all their histories here. Some were essentially studios for hire rather than studios run by and for producers while others rarely rented time to other record producers. Some of the most revered producers actually made the bulk of their groundbreaking work before they built their own studio: Bunny 'Striker' Lee only got his studio up and running after creating his best selling records. Many of the most prolific and innovative producers, Prince Buster and Augustus Pablo for example, never operated their own studios but were often inextricably linked with a particular studio. Nothing beats hearing the music and this is not an academic treatise describing and analysing this as we feel the music speaks for itself. Nor is it a detailed catalogue of every last piece of equipment in Kingston's recording studios and neither does it relate the life stories of the artists. Many influential performers might only get a brief mention while producers who never operated their own studios are only mentioned in passing despite their important contributions to the development of the music.

The majority of the histories of reggae music have been written after Bob Marley's international breakthrough and everything was viewed from a very different perspective before this. It was important to initially rely on the handful of people who were actually interviewing people and writing seriously about the music at the time it was being made such as Carl Gayle, Dave Hendley and Chris Lane. Many peripheral figures have had time over the ensuing years to work on their stories and place themselves nearer to the centre stage while major players have perhaps had more important things to do than work on their Bob Marley recollections, name every musician on a session or compile a list of their releases in chronological order.

I once asked Burning Spear about 'The Prophet', a deejay cut by Big Joe to one of his own productions for his Spear label, a version to 'Throw Down Your Arms' credited to Big Joe & Burning Spear, hoping to include it on a proposed compilation. He had no recollection of meeting the deejay or of recording the song.

"What label is it on?"
"Your label. Spear"
"My label? Are you sure?"
"I have a copy here"
"But I've never met Big Joe…"

And, while working on another compilation another producer and artist, who shall remain nameless, recalled his first recording session in Kingston:

"So we went upstairs to Joe Gibbs' studio on North Parade with Sylvan Morris at the controls…"

"But Joe Gibbs' studio was on Retirement Crescent. Do you mean upstairs at Randy's studio?"
"Yeah… it was Randy's studio"
"And Sylvan Morris was working the board?"
"Yeah..."
"Are you sure it wasn't Errol T?"
"Yeah ... it was Errol T."

But it is too easy to slip into 'train spotting' mode. The artists, musicians and producers made the music and then moved on to their next piece of work. Can you recall exactly what you were doing forty years ago to the day? And who you were with at the time? An outsider will, supposedly, have a more objective view than an insider but it does not necessarily mean that there is any actual insight. This is not a new phenomenon.

"Many were amazed at the knowledge displayed by collectors. In 1949 Louis Armstrong set foot in this country (UK) en route to play a festival in Nice. Among the host of worshippers who arrived at London Airport was an intrepid journalist and collector determined to discover if Louis had played on an obscure record made in 1930 called 'Blue Yodel No. 9' recorded by hillbilly singer Jimmie Rodgers. The journalist was Max Jones, who brought a wind up gramophone to the VIP's room, sat before an astonished Armstrong and played him the record. It was a unique situation. Here was a major artiste of our time, with an international reputation, confronted by a journalist armed with a portable gramophone and a box of steel needles. Louis declared he was on the record and another entry went firmly into the Armstrong discography. The Melody Maker proudly headlined their 'Collector's Corner' column CORNER SCOOPS WORLD ON 1930 ARMSTRONG DISC."
Jim Godbolt

Bunny 'Striker' Lee, whose almost total recall and attention to detail are as impressive as his prolific catalogue, proved, as always, particularly helpful with this project.

"Some of the people don't really **know** the story. Some of the people… they just really **get** the story… they don't **know** it… but I was there from the beginning. This month (August 2006) I will be sixty five so I'm around a long time. I don't propagate any of this. I **know**... I know these things 'cause I was there in the midst of everything.

And there's more… I just have to remember. 1966 is so long ago and I don't remember everything. But from I first came into this I was like an encyclopaedia within the music. Mrs Pottinger used to call me 'The ghost that haunts the studios'…" **Bunny 'Striker' Lee**

Respect and gratitude must also be given to Roy Cousins of The Royals for his recollections, his unfailing good humour, help and advice and for allowing us to use a selection of his extensive memorabilia in these pages.

"A lot of things have gone on in the business but no-one has ever asked me and a lot of people give interviews to big them chest up when they weren't there. They don't know… you understand me? They have nothing to do with it… that's the reason when you write the book I give it my blessing. I've seen so much documentary on television by people who are talking things they don't know about. They weren't there. Me can tell you about Bob Marley. Me can tell you about Delroy Wilson. Me can tell you about The Heptones… all of them man because I was there. It's not fiction! I was there… but I'm not bigging up myself. Please don't think that." **Roy Cousins**

A pronounced anti-establishment element is often prevalent in popular music and there is a received wisdom that defines all Jamaican music as protest music or 'rebel music' with an accompanying 'black power' message. This is, of course, due to the worldwide popularity of Bob Marley and the protestations over the years from some of the leading proponents of this strand within the music, including Bob Marley himself, have done little to dispel this particular myth.

"Reggae doesn't have to be political, or angry. It can be about anything. Most things are worth making music about." **Bob Marley**

"I and I no sing to make anyone believe in Selassie or whatever I defend. I and I sing to make people think any way they want to think. I and I just sing what I know to be the right thing. See so you no have to believe in what I believe to understand the music." **Burning Spear**

"I believe in freedom for everyone, not just the black man."
Bob Marley

The history of Jamaican music abounds with the names of many stars, hugely popular in their own era and in their own way, who are now largely forgotten because their reputations were not consolidated outside the confines of the music at the time. When it finally gained international recognition in the mid-Seventies their vital contributions were unjustly overlooked. Many important performers were ignored because they lacked the necessary image and failed to come up to the expectations of the new audience whose attraction to reggae was often based on a romanticised ideal of Rastafarian mysticism. Genuine talent was overlooked in favour of the 'correct' cultural credentials. Many artists and musicians who had helped shape the direction and content of Jamaican music in the previous decade were ignored and ultimately consigned to oblivion. The famously fickle reggae audience, always on the lookout for this week's sensation, were probably partly to blame but the real reasons are as complex and contradictory as the history of the music itself. Anomalies also arose as many of the music's biggest crossover hits were not only not made by its biggest stars but were also atypical of what was happening at the time in the reggae world. This gave rise to another school of thought that decreed that the music was little more than a novelty. However, listening to the records played on Radio 1 and that made the UK National Charts, such as 'Long Shot Kick The/De Bucket', 'Irie Feelings', 'Dat' & 'Up Town Top Ranking', without any knowledge of the records' background or the people who made them, it might be difficult to draw any other conclusion.

The popularity of American rhythm & blues in Jamaica in the late Forties and early Fifties inspired the phenomenon of the sound system and the power of this music, when played on one of the top sounds, was so moving that it took on an almost physical presence. Amplifiers, speaker boxes and steel horns would be painstakingly assembled and bass and treble frequencies carefully balanced to make the sound just right. Throughout the Fifties the sound system operators fought to keep ahead of the opposition by playing the most exclusive American 78rpm records to their fiercely partisan followers. As the decade progressed the preferred style of music in the USA gradually changed and an altogether smoother, some would say bland, approach began to find favour with American audiences. The supplies of tough, driving rhythm & blues began to dwindle and the more forward thinking sound system owners began to record their own 'transcription discs' to maintain their pre-eminence in the dance halls.

The operators approached accomplished musicians, Jamaica's jazz, big band and orchestra dance elite, to fulfil their musical needs. The musical explosion that ensued was built around their recreation of a style of music that had now outrun its 'usefulness' in its original habitat. Initially these one off custom cut discs, or acetates, were played solely on their sets but they proved so popular with their followers and the demand so great that the operators began to release their music commercially. Instead of reproducing the sound of someone else's records they became record producers. The entire history of this massively influential form consists of many similar fortunate incidents or accidents, "every spoil is a style", and making a record, as opposed to making music, is one of the most critical factors in the development of reggae music. Consequently the role of record producer is pivotal to this narrative; they have commanded a central role in the history of Jamaican music despite the fact that, more often than not, they were not present on many of 'their' recording sessions. The name of the producer on a record indicates the man who paid for and set up the session regardless of his musical understanding or technical ability.

"You used to have Joe Gibbs & The Professionals and the people don't know who played the music. Joe Gibbs, like myself, couldn't play a note."
Bunny 'Striker' Lee

"In effect they (the producers) were like film directors controlling the crucial aspects of production to impose their vision…"
Steve Barrow & Peter Dalton

The producer was the vital catalyst that caused the records to be made rather than the person who made the records. This is not to denigrate their many achievements, the musicians are more than capable of doing that, but to attempt to place the role of producer in its correct context.

"Most of the producers well… it's really musicians who make the music. They build up a different vibe. Me name musician and them only name producer."
Augustus Pablo

"I just call them record backers. They just have the money to make a record and to make more money. They don't know anything about the music and we make the tunes for them. They're too interested in the money."   **Winston Wright**

"Then we found we had been doing the work for all of the hit making producers and the term 'producer' had been misunderstood in Jamaica. Many times the executive producers were getting credits for musical production when we were doing the work and they weren't even around. We were the musicians on their products and many times the actual producers but not credited as producers. That's how it's always been in reggae…

More of the producers should be credited as the executive producers. You find that most of the work is done by the engineer and the musicians."
Cleveland 'Clevie' Brownie

"You get some of them who hire you for a session and they expect you to make it up for them sometimes. Even if they have a tune you still have to work out the chords and arrangements for yourself. After that you have to make a bridge for the tune. Sometimes though a producer might tell you to do something but it probably doesn't sound any good so you've got to cut it out without him noticing! That's the trouble with these producers… they can't play any instruments… not even a tambourine."
Winston Wright

The first record producers from the sound systems were not over concerned with who the musicians or singers were or how they might sound or look on a stage show but only with how effective a record would be when played on their sound. This attitude was to influence all that followed. In most other genres of music the accepted route was for bands or singers to come together to make music and then consider making a record but in Jamaica the sound system men irrevocably altered this process.

"A long time me a singer me no sing no hit
Give me little rhythm make me sing one quick
This is the studio and I man have this sound
Come now music man make me mash up the land

I want to sing a hit song. It's been so long
I want to sing a hit song. Don't keep me down
I want to sing a hit song. It's been so long
I want to sing a hit song…

Every day I get up I look into the world
I see big cars. I see pretty girls
I'll be a better man if I had money in my hand
Help me oh Jah I want to come on strong

I want to sing a hit song. It's been so long
I want to sing a hit song. Don't keep me down
I want to sing a hit song. It's been so long
I want to sing a hit song…
Sing a hit song
I want to sing a hit song…"

'Hit Song' Roman Stewart

Dillinger's deejay version then expanded the theme…

"Me say me go a Channel One fe go sing a little song
Me sing a little song and them say 'A hit song!'
The natty sings a hit song…

Me say me go a Randy's fe do a little thing
Me do a little thing it keep you rocking and swing
The natty sings a hit song…

Me say me go a Treasure Isle fe go pop little style
Me pop a little style and them said fe rest a while
The natty sings a hit song…

Me say me go a Harry J fe go get my pay
I get my pay and I walked away
The natty sings a hit song…

Me say me go a Channel One fe go do another song
Me do another song them say me can't be wrong
The natty sings a hit song…

Introduction

I man go up a Talent Corporation
Just to make a penetration
Up a Talent Corporation
And to give them my vibration
To hit them with a rocking vibration
And to treat the generation
With this musical inspiration…"

'Natty Sings A Hit Song' Dillinger

It is difficult to now resist the temptation to look for a pattern where none existed; to see a logical, linear development with the benefit of hindsight and subsequently attained insight: to expound on the significance of certain key records and to put everything in its place in a neatly ordered chronological format. It is also worth pointing out that most artists, musicians and producers will tell you they were the first to make an actual ska record, to make a proper rock steady record, to make a real reggae record or to release a dub album but this is not of critical importance. Many people were doing similar things at the same time at different stages of the music's development so claims of 'the first' and 'the original' have been retained. It is now impossible to say for certain who was the first and, in the end, does it really matter? Nothing can ever exist in a vacuum and things are not necessarily as they seem to be. Often what have become the accepted 'facts' are not the facts at all.

"It's the way you a go look 'pon it now! You see it like a pattern and a time. You can't look 'pon it so…" **Augustus Pablo**

Some of the producer's stories effectively start at the opening of their studio while others seem to come to an abrupt end at this point. Certain studios are far better known for the work of other producers and not that of their owners: King Tubby did not 'produce' records, even within the Jamaican definition, until the Eighties and, even then, he encouraged other, younger men, do the work. The two most successful record producers, and studio proprietors, of the Sixties, Duke Reid and Coxsone Dodd, usually entrusted the day to day running of their studios to their musicians and engineers. Alongside the many incredible achievements are stories of lost opportunities such as King Tubby winding transformers and mending television sets or Herman Chin-Loy remaining behind the counter of his shop selling records. Some might well be contradictory but, as Augustus

Pablo stated, that there is no pattern, and often no rhyme or reason to the "half that's never been told…"

"About two years ago the Jamaican entertainment scene became alive as a result of the forward strides made in one of Jamaica's newest industries - the record manufacturing field. The record industry presented the local artistes a showcase for his talents and the opportunity of assessing himself." **Sonny Bradshaw**

If people can't hear the music then it means nothing. But at what point does commerce become commercialisation? The same old uptown vs downtown, business vs creativity and then baldheads vs dreadlocks arguments have never ceased and still continue but the development of a viable infrastructure was essential to the development and growth of Jamaican music. This is how it happened…

Naoki Ienaga

Chapter 1
How It All Began: Motta's Recording Studio

"Yes, there is music everywhere in Jamaica. It pulses in the traffic of the streets, where the brazen voices of modern auto horns argue with the sharp, sudden accents of the donkey driver; it is in the quiet avenues of the suburbs where modern houses sprawl on cool green grounds; it is in the teeming slums where the crowded population finds expression in laughter, and in the provocative music story of the island."
'MRS Authentic Jamaican Calypsos'

Mention Jamaican music and most people will immediately think of reggae. Anyone with more than a passing interest in the subject will tell you that its roots are in American rhythm & blues from which Jamaican rhythm & blues (also known as shuffle and boogie), ska, rock steady and reggae all developed but the music known as mento has, until comparatively recently, been the sole preserve of musical scholars. The mento recordings of Stanley Motta were the beginnings of a musical phenomenon whose influence would eventually reach all around the world and back again.

"Calypso and mento and a thing named quadrille are a part of Jamaican music that people don't talk about. We started with mento and the old folks, like my mum and dad, they called it quadrille with the first and second figures. Some people say quadrille came from France but I don't know... some people say it came from England in Oliver Cromwell's time. Others say Spain so they don't know and that part of it I can't tell you about! But with quadrille and mento music they changed the name to calypso then it came right down to soca. These things don't stay still. They keep on moving and I don't know what name they're going to come with next! But the original Jamaican roots music like mento and calypso they're still here and they're still in demand. The original mento bands with their rhumba boxes with guys like Count Lasher... those people are dead now and they're only now starting to get recognition because people now have started looking back on this music and saying 'Well, this music was great music!'" **Bunny 'Striker' Lee**

Before Stanley Beresford Brandon Motta (5th October 1915 to 22nd March 1993) opened his recording studio on Hanover Street in downtown Kingston in 1951 and began cutting mento sides by local artists there was no indigenous Jamaican recording business.

"The only recording that was done in those days was by Motta's Recording Studio. Stanley Motta had a dealership for radio and electronics and somehow or other he managed to hack together a disc recorder with I think, at best, two microphones... and that was the only recording."
Graeme Goodall

"Our recording studio was not what you'd call a recording studio now. It was a back room in the woodwork factory, twelve or fourteen feet square, with insulated soft ceiling boards. The band and the recording equipment were all in the same room and there was one microphone. All there was on the cutting machine was one volume control knob." **Brian Motta**

Mento was usually performed by small groups of musicians playing banjo, guitar, fife, maracas and a 'rhumba box', a plucked box instrument usually home made, used to play simple bass lines which originated from the African mbira, and also known as the marimbula, bass kalimba, or thumb piano. It was occasionally augmented by a bamboo saxophone and violin and, in its later urban based context, violin, clarinet, saxophone and piano were also included. The origins of mento can, naturally enough, be found in Africa but the music also demonstrates considerable European influences. The European quadrille dance was introduced to

Jamaica by the plantation owners and their African slaves would play the music on fifes and fiddles (violins).

"The heyday of the quadrille was from 1880 to 1900. A complicated dance with formal and regular patterns, the quadrille passed from the salons of the Second French Empire to the provinces, and thence abroad."
Earl Leaf

After emancipation in 1838 the quadrille split into the more formal ballroom style that was favoured by high society and what became known as the camp style which incorporated African elements. Both styles of quadrille consisted of five 'figures' beginning slowly with the first figure and with the pace quickening gradually up until the fifth and fastest figure. Anthropologists have claimed that it was the appropriation of the quadrille by the emancipated Jamaican slaves of the far freer camp style, and the fifth figure in particular, that eventually gave birth to mento.

Following the migration of country people to Kingston in the Forties mento moved to the city where it often became the backing for highly erotic dance performances in Kingston's bars and nightclubs. Its lyrical content was never as innuendo ridden as Trinidadian calypso although sex was, naturally enough, a favourite topic. The lyrics were usually wry and often humorous accounts of everyday life in both the countryside and the town.

"Calypso can be gay, mischievous, critical and honestly naughty and has always served as a means of communication in the West Indies, 'reporting' on every aspect of life imaginable from the weather to world affairs; the latest births and deaths to the current trend in politics…"
'Independence Jump Up Calypso'

"Then there is the music that is peculiarly Jamaican – the mento. This is the specific tempo of the island. The result of the meeting of Afro-Latin influences is a distinctive beat and rhythm in the music of Jamaica that identifies it to the tuned ear."   **'Authentic Jamaican Calypsos'**

It was a live music and the city musicians would add more 'modern' instruments to fill out the sound as they played in the hotels and nightclubs. At the time most Jamaican nightclubs were only open on Saturdays and there were limited opportunities for musicians to play live. Consequently,

many of the island's top jazz musicians such as Wilton Gaynair, Joe Harriott, Bertie King and Dizzy Reece left the island for the UK and the USA. Those that remained played the sort of music that positively encouraged lascivious dancing and their approach was markedly different to the more restrained traditional rural forms of the music.

The dance company formed by Harold 'Harry Biggs' Holness and Daisy Riley became the leading dance act in nightclubs such as the Wickie Wackie Beach Club or the Midway Club and they would often perform at several clubs a night. Holness and Riley and their troupe would entertain the crowds at establishments such as the Stony Hill Club where the resident band, led by George Moxey with Ben Bowers as Master of Ceremonies, played a mixture of swing, jive and mento. It was this band that formed the nucleus of Stanley Motta's house band for his pioneering Jamaican recording company. They would play alongside outfits formed by the legendary Baba Motta (no relation to Stanley) a piano-playing luminary of the Kingston jazz and dance band scene who, over the years, had employed guitarist Ernest Ranglin and saxophonists Roland Alphonso and Lester Sterling in his band.

"I played with Baba Motta for a while. We were the first people to open Montego Beach Hotel..." **Ernest Ranglin**

From as early as 1912 the music of Trinidad had enjoyed considerable international success and the Trinidadian bandleader, Sam Manning, covered traditional songs such as 'Hold 'Im Joe' for Columbia Records as far back as the Twenties. Trinidadian calypso records were sold in Jamaica through outlets such as Campbell's Record Shop on King Street, however, the music of Jamaica remained largely ignored until Jamaican 'national treasure' and folklorist 'Miss Lou' (Louise Bennett) made a handful of recordings for the London based Melodisc label in late 1950 that included her interpretations of 'Linstead Market' and 'Wheel And Turn Me'.

"Why was it just (the music from) Trinidad that got so well known at the time? Lord Kitchener came to England and did a lot of songs and the music caught on up here. He was a Trinidadian and he carried the banner. He was the king of calypso so Trinidad took it like their national music..." **Bunny 'Striker' Lee**

By the time Stanley Motta began to make his first recordings an incredibly wide variety of differing influences had been assimilated by Jamaican musicians. The popularity of dance bands meant that instruments such as clarinets, saxophones, drums and pianos were incorporated into the line up of local bands. Other factors exerted varying degrees of influence: the omnipresent radio beaming in from the USA and Cuba, the increasing availability of imported records, the presence of the US military in the Caribbean and the steady flow of Jamaican seasonal emigrant labour to the USA, Cuba, Panama and Nicaragua all contributed to the development of the music.

Throughout the history of the island it is important to never forget the Jamaican motto, Out Of Many We Are One, and that the population of Jamaica consisted of many different races and classes.

"Jamaicans are proud of their music. They are proud because in the distinctive beat of their music lies all their own history. Here is the musical meeting ground of the African, the Indian and Chinese, the English, Welsh, Irish, Scots, the Portuguese and Spanish, in fact, all the varied people who are hidden behind the designation 'Jamaican'."
'MRS Authentic Jamaican Calypsos'

"The Spanish seemed to have an influence on the style of calypsos in Jamaica which are of a rhythm called 'mento'. It is infectious and today it is becoming more popular than ever." **'Meet Me In Jamaica'**

Sephardic Jews, originally from Spain and Portugal, had lived in Jamaica since the sixteenth century when the Spanish had first occupied the island. The Mottas were an old, established and highly regarded family of Sephardic Jews. Stanley Motta was a member of the Kingston Chamber Of Commerce, The Jamaican Tourist Board, The Board Of The Bank Of Jamaica and President and Director of The United Congregation of Israelites on Duke Street in Kingston. Stanley Motta had four sons: David, now living in Australia, Phillip and Robert, both now living in the USA, and Brian who lives in Canada. This pillar of the Jamaican establishment devoted much of his life to promoting and marketing the music of Jamaica at home and abroad.

"My father was known as 'Fifty Cycle Motta' as he was a driving force in getting the cycle changed from the forty cycle current and, because of the proximity of the USA, the government went to the US cycle."
Brian Motta

Stanley Motta had started work as an apprentice in his uncle's garage business before opening his first electrical spares and appliance shop in 1933 at 10C East Street in Kingston. He later moved premises to the north side of Harbour Street in the heart of Kingston's downtown commercial district. Brian, who was born in 1937, recalled that "two of the major things that carried the business through the war years" of 1939 to 1945 when nothing could be imported were the eight or ten jukeboxes that his father owned and that were sited at various clubs round Kingston. Stanley Motta sold and operated PA (Public Address) equipment and would rent turntables, amplifiers, speakers and even records for parties. He ran the PA at Knutsford Park (now Caymanas Park) horse races every Saturday: "I remember going with him to check if it was working. Political rallies and private home parties. It all helped."

"The main store was at 109 Harbour Street (the third location) and my father was the distributor for Kodak for umpteen years. There was a big photographic department firstly stocked with cameras from Europe and then cameras from Japan. He was the distributor for Sony when Sony only made two transistor radios! Hoover was another big brand... we sold all their products. We also sold Leak amplifiers, Wharfedale speakers and Garrard record decks."
Brian Motta

From as far back as Brian could remember his father's hobbies were photography and popular and classical music. He was a hi-fi fanatic, "a real gadget man", and when he obtained his first stereo amplifier he "invited all his friends round to listen to it". Brian recalled his father having a recording machine at his Bar Mitzvah (the Jewish coming of age ceremony) in 1950/51 where all the children present were singing into it.

"The recordings were made by cutting on to blank acetates. They could only be played back once using a light pick-up head. If you played them more than a couple of times they began to wear out."
Brian Motta

Chapter 1

Paul Coote

Paul Coote

YOU CAN GET THESE CALYPSOS ON LONG PLAYING RECORDS ALSO
FROM

stanley motta ltd

109 HARBOUR STREET, KINGSTON,
JAMAICA, B.W.I.

The woodwork factory on Hanover Street, "woodwork was another one of dad's hobbies", originally manufactured "gifts in wood" such as picture frames and cigarette boxes for the tourist market. "All kind of different designs were made and sold in the shop." Stanley Motta would put together imported components such as Ecko radios, Garrard decks and speakers and house them in custom made radiograms built from local wood. Radios and record players were still regarded primarily as pieces of furniture and a Motta's radiogram was beautiful to behold. In 1956 the woodwork factory was sold to the Polio Rehabilitation Centre at Mona, a suburb of Kingston, as a teaching and fund raising project for the Centre.

"I can remember quite vividly on one of Winston Churchill's visits to Jamaica that my father was given the job of making a presentation cigar box for him using different coloured woods to make the Union Jack on the lid. But when I went down to deliver it the people said 'I'm sorry to tell you that the flag is wrong'. Apparently the diagonal cross lined up. 'that's alright,' said Stanley Motta, 'you can pick it up in the morning' and the woodworking men spent the night changing it." **Brian Motta**

The record department in Motta's sold records imported from North America and England and, although he advertised 'USA rhythm & blues' in The Daily Gleaner, Stanley Motta was always a staunch supporter of local music. He sold PA Systems to the hotels and "a lot of the time he would go round to install the equipment himself." It was while working on the installations that he heard the hotel bands and the idea came to him for "recording these fellows" and commit their music to posterity.

"That's what the tourists wanted! A good mento singer would stand in front and while he was singing he would make up words to fit the people in the crowd. I was so impressed with these guys singing about the people in the audience." **Brian Motta**

In 1951 Stanley Motta built a small recording studio when he installed a Reslo ribbon microphone and a Presto desktop disc recorder at 93 Hanover Street around the corner from his shop on Harbour Street. Although guitar maestro Ernest Ranglin remembers recording Hawaiian style guitar music directly on to wax cylinders for an unnamed entrepreneur some time before this he recalled that "it wasn't for commercial purposes" and the credit for the first ever Jamaican record goes to a medley of mento

Chapter 1

songs sung by Lord Fly; Stanley Motta was the pioneer who recorded and released it.

MRS Motta's Recording Studio Serial No 01A
'Medley Of Jamaican Mento-Calypsos'
Fan Me Solja Man Fan Me; One Solja Man;
Yuh No Yeary Weh De Ole Man Say; Slide Mongoose
Played by Dan Williams and his Orchestra. Vocal: Lord Fly

MRS Motta's Recording Studio Serial No 01B 'Whai Whai Whai'
Played by Dan Williams and his Orchestra. Vocal: Lord Fly

From these modest beginnings an industry began that would not only bring the talent, experiences and emotions of the Jamaican people to the world but that would also exert an incalculable, incredible influence on the popular music of the latter half of the twentieth century.

The music was cut directly on to 78rpm lacquers, thin aluminium discs coated with soft acetate (a cellulose lacquer), and, as there were no manufacturing facilities on the island, these lacquers were sent to England for mastering and pressing by Decca Records in London. When completed, the fragile shellac 78rpm records were shipped back to Jamaica. Stanley Motta had made the connection with Decca through respected Jamaican jazz musician Bertie King who had lived in London since 1935 but returned to Jamaica in late 1951 to lead a band at the Hotel Casablanca in Montego Bay.

"At first we used the cutting lathe and an aluminium disc coated with acetate on one side only. You needed a special cutting needle to fit into the head and the head tracked across the grooves. You also had to scroll across to make the intro and run out grooves and, if the band made a mistake, you had to stop the machine, throw the acetate away and start again…" **Brian Motta**

Although the original musicians had come from the hotels it soon became known throughout the musical fraternity that Stanley Motta was making records. Right from the start there was an issue with publishing, a business difficulty that has remained with Jamaican music ever since.

"Eventually local musicians would come to us saying 'I have a tune' and my father would have to decide whether to cut it or not depending on whether it could sell or not. We'd have to be careful that they'd written the songs as they were paid outright for the tunes. There were no royalties or publishing agreements." **Brian Motta**

Once the studio was properly established Frank Geoffrey was trained to run it. Frank would then make the decision if a recording was good enough and would decide whether to go ahead and press or not but "there were lots of things that never got past this stage" explained Brian. The cutter was later replaced with a mono reel to reel tape recorder and between 1951 and 1957 the MRS (Motta's Recording Studio) label would go on to release over fifty 78's, a handful of seven inch 45's, five ten inch LPs and three twelve inch albums. Stanley Motta also licensed a selection of his material to Hart's in Montego Bay for tourists but his advertisements in The Daily Gleaner were still aimed directly at the local market.

"MRS Jamaica Calypsos. The Liveliest Notes for your Christmas Party! At the top of the list: played by The Ticklers 'Glamour Gal' the other side of 'Don't Fence Her In'... MRS Records Now Only 6/6."

Ivan Chin, Ken Khouri and Edward Seaga "before he got into his political career" all "got into it in a far bigger way", Brian recalled, although by 1957 the popularity of mento had faded and "sales were not there anymore in Jamaica. All of the Motta's stores had record departments but I can't remember selling any mento at all." Mento continued to sell in England, where Stanley Motta had set up licensing deals with Emil Shallit's Melodisc label and London Records but, by the time the decade drew to a close, interest in mento was almost non-existent in Jamaica. Emil Shallit would go on to license Jamaican rhythm & blues and ska recordings for UK release on his influential Blue Beat label.

Motta's Recording Studio also played a small, but highly significant role, in the creation of Jamaican rhythm & blues and some of Laurel Aitken's earliest recordings were cut on Harbour Street. Laurel had moved from Cuba to Jamaica in 1938 and started his musical career performing mento and calypso songs to visitors as they alighted from the cruise ships moored in Kingston Harbour. He would go on to play an important, if still undervalued, role in the development of Jamaican music in Jamaica and the UK.

"Laurel Aitken never get any recognition either. He should have got an OD before he passed away. His parents were Jamaican but he was born in Cuba. He had two brothers... one was a barber and the other was the great guitarist Bobby Aitken. These guys really did something for Jamaican music."
Bunny 'Striker' Lee

Singer and record producer Derrick Harriott recalled going to Stanley Motta's "sometime in 1956 or 1957" to record the original self financed acetate of 'Lollipop Girl' where Claude Sang played the piano, "just a piano a play the rhythm",while they both handled the vocal duties: "There were no tracks, no console board. You started singing and that's how we made 'Lollipop Girl'." Derrick then gave the 'transcription disc' to Thunderbird Sound, a Maxfield Avenue sound system, "who used to run a Friday night after work session." Thunderbird Sound would "sometimes play it up to ten times in a row... the crowd loved the song so much they wouldn't let the deejay take it off". There was a huge amount of interest in the disc and Duke Reid and Coxsone, the two undisputed top sound systems of the time, soon heard about 'Lollipop Girl'. Coxsone exchanged it for "one of his big American hits... and it became an even bigger hit on Coxsone's Downbeat Sound". Not long afterwards Derrick Harriott recalled "Duke Reid played back the dub against Coxsone at the Mizpah Hall opposite The Gaiety Theatre. Guns were drawn! Only Coxsone was supposed to have it!" Apparently one of Coxsone's operators had appropriated the original acetate and had another copy cut from it. "'Lollipop Girl' started so many conflicts" and, when Derrick, re-recorded 'Lollipop Girl' for Duke Reid as one of The Jiving Juniors in 1960, accompanied this time by Duke Reid And His Group, it would become one of Jamaica's best loved songs.

"You could go to a dance and hear 'Lollipop Girl' fifteen times straight. People didn't want it to come off the set you know!" **Derrick Harriott**

The last album released on the Motta's label was 'An Afternoon At Hope Gardens, Jamaica, British West Indies with the Jamaica Military Band'. The selection included interpretations of mento favourites such as 'Linstead Market', 'Brown Skin Gal' and 'Hol' 'Im Joe' recorded at the RJR studio with Graeme Goodall.

"We pressed some on $33^{1/3}$ rpm and some 45's but by then we'd finished with the 78's. We made some long playing records but they were put together in England using our original masters. The last recording we did was a twelve inch LP of the Jamaican Military Band in 1957. There were far too many of them to fit in the Motta's Recording Studio so we rented the RJR studio and they did the cutting too. This was the last release on MRS… I'm pretty sure it's the last one we did." **Brian Motta**

After Stanley Motta had stopped recording local artists his electrical business continued to flourish until he retired in 1986 and sold it to Mussori Limited but the Mottas' influence on Jamaican music had not quite finished. Brian Motta went on to work with Byron Lee as a photographer and his work graces the covers of many of Byron Lee's albums. He also "toured the islands" with Byron Lee & The Dragonaires in the early Sixties.

Stanley Motta deserves far more than a footnote in the history of Jamaican music. In fact most histories of reggae and its forerunners do not mention his name at all although he was the first Jamaican to record local artists and to promote their music internationally. His recordings used the island's top bands who had perfected their art on the nightclub and hotel circuits and featured the island's best vocalists of the period. His catalogue contains some of the greatest examples of rural and urban mento styles and the artwork and designs for his label and sleeves were always world class. By presenting this relatively esoteric art form in such a sophisticated style he enabled it to reach an international audience.

Motta's Recording Studio established the template for the Jamaican recording business for the remainder of the century: always work with the best home grown talent and, in addition to the 'local' market, never forget the international market of both the expatriate Jamaican community and the all important 'foreign' element. It was due to Stanley Motta's vision and hard work that the very real qualities of what was once sneeringly referred to by members of the more privileged sections of Jamaican society as "gardener boy music" would become recognised and acknowledged worldwide.

Motta's Recording Studio
93 Hanover Street
Kingston

Producers, Arrangers & Engineers include:
Stanley Motta, Donald Hendry, Frank Geoffrey & Jim Taylor

Labels:
MRS (Motta's Recording Studio)

Musicians:
Charlie Binger & His Quintet
Lord Composer & The Silver Seas Orchestra
Lord Composer & His Silver Seas Hotel Orchestra
Lord Composer & The Silver Seas Orchestra
Count Lasher & His Quintet
Lord Messam & His Calypsonians
Baba Motta & His Orchestra
Baba Motta & His Jamaicans
George Moxey & His Calypso Quintet
George Moxey Quartet
Count Owen & His Calypsonians
Mapletoft Poulle
Reynold's Calypso Clippers (Tenor Banjo: Eddie Brown)
Monty Reynolds & The Shaw Park Calypso Band
Monty Reynolds & His Silver Seas Hotel Orchestra
Harold Richardson & The Ticklers
Dan Williams & His Orchestra
Vocalists: Ben Bower, Eddie Brown, Boysie Grant, Clyde Hoyte, Peter Hudson, Lord Fly (Bertie Lyons), Baba Motta, Hubert Porter & Harold Richardson

Chapter 2

Paul Coote

Chapter 2
Mento Gets Another Mention
Chin's Radio Services
&
The Caribbean Recording Company Ltd

"Then there is the music that is particularly Jamaican – the mento. This is the specific tempo of the island."
'MRS Authentic Jamaican Calypsos'

"We started with mento music and you had Chin's and Stanley Motta's. Mento come out through Stanley Motta's, Chin's Records and 'Baba'/'Dada' Tewari…" **Bunny 'Striker' Lee**

"So I personally feel that mento had more influence on it than anything else…" **Graeme Goodall**

"In the early years some of the sounds would play mento… the first Jamaican music. It's still popular in Jamaica. It captures a rural feel more than any other sound and a mento based record still outsells any other record in Jamaica!" **Winston 'Merritone' Blake**

"It is my strong belief that Jamaican dancers still carry a deep affection for mento and if they heard enough of it we could aid in the revival of our National Folklore." **Carlos Malcolm**

Other enterprising entrepreneurs, including Ivan S Chin and 'Baba' aka 'Dada' Tewari, followed Stanley Motta and began recording and releasing mento records during the Fifties. Their work within the genre would play another important role in the foundation of the Jamaican recording industry.

Ivan Samuel Chin was a stalwart pioneer and champion of Jamaican music. Born 4th April 1924 in Kingston, his mother came from India and his father was from China and Ivan grew up steeped in Chinese culture in Montego Bay on Jamaica's North Coast. He became fascinated with radio as a young man and studied electronics by post through one of the many courses available. Ivan enrolled with the 'Learn Radio By Correspondence Course' run by the Hollywood Radio & Television Institute in Los Angeles, California and the cost of the course was one pound a month.

After opening his first radio repair business in Montego Bay in 1942 Ivan moved to New York for a short while in the winter of 1946. "I never knew what cold was until I felt my first winter and saw my first snow" and he returned to Jamaica in 1947. The following year Ivan married Lily Chuck. Lily was unaware of the influence the fledgling Jamaican music industry was to have on their lives together but the arrival of Ken Khouri (see Chapter 4), another pioneering record producer, carrying a piece of bulky equipment at her wedding to Ivan might possibly have given her a clue.

"That disc recorder that Ken Khouri bought in Miami was used to record our wedding ceremony. Ken took it to the church and set it up for the first time to do a wedding... even the Minister was confused." **Ivan Chin**

Ivan opened Chin's Radio Service at 48 Church Street in Kingston "a few years later". The shop started off doing repairs and "this was the main business". He also sold records and, after two years, went into the sale of Grundig, Ecko and Pye radios, batteries and large electrical appliances. He then purchased Ken Khouri's Presto disc recorder and began using it to make his own mento recordings "in the store... the floor was concrete and the ceiling Gypsum. There were no (sound) acoustic rooms". These

78rpm releases on the Chin's label proudly boasted 'Pressed Exclusively For Chin's Radio Service' and, as well as records on his own label, the store also sold:

"Motta's and Khouri's records too. But there was not much money in it as the records sold at three shillings and sixpence (seventeen and a half pence) each. I never thought they would still be selling now... the originals sell at very high prices."
Ivan Chin

Ivan recalls that he did not regard Chin's as being in competition with Motta's because "we were all in it together" and, as the business expanded, he opened more stores culminating in eight in total "all round the island". In 1955 he "discovered two local musicians", Everart Williams and Alerth Bedasse, and invited their quintet to record exclusively for Chin's.

"I changed their name from Calypso Quintet to Chin's Calypso Sextet. Alerth Bedasse was the song composer and singer and Everart Williams was the lyrics composer. Bedasse was the man who put the band together and directed the men. He also composed the melody for each of the songs with them. Williams was very intelligent and manager of the band. The first two records I did were 'Honeymoon', 'Rough Rider' 'Samson And Delilah' and 'Depression' He was also a great and talented composer. Once I engaged the fellows exclusively I was committed to make two records a month."
Ivan Chin

Chin's Calypso Sextet rehearsed and recorded in "a section of the store at nights after the store was closed" and Ivan recorded them directly on to acetate lacquers "using a cutting needle to cut grooves into 78rpm ten inch vinyl resin discs. The blank discs were not cheap so we had to use them sparingly". The microphones he used were the "old ribbon types", RCA and Shure, and all the tunes were recorded in the shop on Church Street. There was no studio. "One track. One take. We had to rehearse a lot more to make sure we had it right before cutting". Eventually Ivan bought a Grundig reel to reel tape recorder and his last selection of tunes was recorded in stereo.

"Everart Williams and Alerth Bedasse wrote most of their songs from personal experiences and stories they heard on the streets of Jamaica. Williams was the very best calypso composer for that period and Bedasse

Chapter 2

LEARNING COLOR TV, COMMUNICATIONS, ELECTRONICS IS FAST, EASY, FASCINATING WITH NRI

ALL THIS IS YOURS — from Achievement Kit to Color TV set you build yourself — when you enroll for the NRI TV-Radio Servicing course. Other courses are equally complete. Unique training methods, "bite-size" texts, many personal services have kept NRI the 55-year leader in its field.

ACT NOW—STEP UP TO HIGHER PAY, A BRIGHTER FUTURE
EARN $5 TO $7 AN HOUR SOON AFTER YOU ENROLL

Even if your education is limited, you can learn Color Television Servicing, Communications or Industrial Electronics at home in your spare time the NRI way. NRI has spent millions of dollars simplifying, organizing, dramatizing home study training in this fast growing field — perfecting education at home to make it easy to grasp, entertaining, exciting and practical. The NRI learn-by-doing way trains your hands as well as your head.

Be a skilled technician in America's fastest growing industry Color Television is just one of the money-making "boom" markets in the field of Electronics. And Electronics is growing so fast it is expected to be America's number-one industry in a few short years. TV technicians are in demand now to keep millions of color sets in working order. NRI prepares you with actual on-the-job experience by including in its Color TV course a custom-designed color set totally engineered for training purposes. You learn by *doing*, demonstrating things you read about in "bite-size" texts as you build and work with professional equipment. Electronics comes alive in a fascinating way. In Color TV, the end product is your own high quality set, yours to keep for years of viewing pleasure.

15 NRI TRAINING PLANS give you a choice of fields
NRI has a training plan to fit every interest, every need in Color TV Servicing, Communications, Industrial Electronics. You can learn to be your own boss in your own TV-Radio Servicing business, or make $5 to $7 an hour fixing sets in spare time. Or you can get into the fascinating fields of broadcasting-communications. Or be a part of the Electronics

APPROVED UNDER GI BILL
If you have served since January 31, 1955, or are in service, check GI line in coupon.

"revolution" in business and industry; learn to understand computers; or take part in missile, rocket and satellite programs. Whatever your interest, whatever your need, NRI has fifteen training plans tailored for you.

Act now — get all the facts Opportunities are endless for the well-trained man. Discover the ease and excitement of training at home with the leader — NRI. Mail the coupon today for new NRI color catalog. No obligation. No salesman will call on you. NATIONAL RADIO INSTITUTE, Electronics Division, Washington, D.C. 20016.

FREE COLOR CATALOG

NATIONAL RADIO INSTITUTE
Electronics Division
Washington, D.C. 20016   254-099

Please send me your new catalog. I have checked the field of most interest to me. (No salesman will call.) Please PRINT.

☐ TV-Radio Servicing (with color) ☐ Aircraft Communications
☐ Advanced Color TV ☐ Mobile Communications
☐ Complete Communications ☐ Marine Communications
☐ FCC License ☐ Amateur Radio
☐ Industrial Electronics ☐ Advanced Amateur Radio
☐ Basic Electronics ☐ Electrical Appliance Repair
☐ Math for Technicians ☐ Air conditioning — Refrigeration
☐ Electronics for Automation ☐ **CHECK FOR FACTS ON GI BILL**

Name_____Age_____
Address_____
City_____State_____Zip_____
ACCREDITED MEMBER NATIONAL HOME STUDY COUNCIL

Noel Hawks

was the best calypso songwriter and also a very good singer. They both worked together on each song, line by line, until the words and songs came together in harmony. They were an excellent team. I was very proud of them." **Ivan Chin**

Ivan recalled that his musicians were always very co-operative, very easy to get on with and that "there was no cursing or quarrelling". Everart Williams was not only the composer, arranger and director but also played percussion: maracas and sticks. The Chin's Calypso Sextet's instruments consisted of a rhumba box, a bamboo saxophone, a bamboo flute, a banjo, a guitar, a floor bass guitar with four strings, maracas and two heavy sticks called clave "which they knock together." All the instruments were made in Jamaica using local wood, bamboo "and other things". The saxophone player also played the bamboo flute and Alerth Bedasse sang and played guitar.

The lacquers and the tapes were sent to Decca in London for processing and manufacturing. "It would take about four weeks, or a little more, for the finished records to come back." The business relationship between Chin's Radio Service and Decca was excellent and, when he contacted them in 2003, Ivan was amazed to discover that the company still held his original masters. "Copies of my orders and all the things from the time" that had been kept for half a century in the Decca Library were all then returned to Ivan. "They only usually kept classical records but they'd kept the Chin's records too! The only set they couldn't find was the originals of the later reel to reel recordings."

Some titles on the Chin's label were pressed in very limited quantities of "only four hundred" although some, such as the controversial 'Night Food Recipe', were very big sellers. "The government wanted to ban it because it was bad for the children" but in 1957 Ivan decided to stop making records.

"I said good bye to all the members of the band in June 1957 especially Williams and Bedasse. It was a sad time for everyone because the band was breaking up. There was no work for the band as a complete unit as calypso was going out..." **Ivan Chin**

The CARIBBEAN RECORDING CO. LTD.

takes pleasure in announcing their appointment as

EXCLUSIVE PRESSERS, MANUFACTURERS & DISTRIBUTORS OF PHONOGRAPH RECORDS

in the British West Indies and British Colonial Africa Regions
for the following firms in the United States Of America

- IMPERIAL Records Inc.
- ALADDIN Records Inc.
- INTRO Records Inc.
- CHESS Records Inc.
- ARGO Records Inc.
- CHECKER Records Inc.

- DOOTONE Records Inc.
- UNITED Records Inc.
- STATES Records Inc.
- DUKE Records Inc.
- PEACOCK Records Inc.
- SPECIALTY Records Inc.
- ATLANTIC Records Inc.

- ATCO Records Inc.
- ROOST Records Inc.
- MODERN Records Inc.
- VERNE Records Inc.
- VEEJAY Records Inc.
- AMPAR Records Inc.
- GOTHAM Records Inc.

featuring such popular artists as:

- Fats Domino
- Shirley & Lee
- Lavern Baker
- Marvin & Johnnie
- Smiley Lewis
- Dave Bartholomew
- Gene & Eunice
- Roscoe Gordon

- Johnny Ace
- Al Hibbler
- Louis Jordan
- Spiders
- Joe Liggins
- Big Walter
- Twilighters
- Lynn Hope
- David Hill

- Joe Turner
- Ernie Freeman
- Bonnemere
- Eddie "Lockjaw" Davis
- Lloyd Price
- Tab Smith
- The Blockbusters
- Little Richard

THE CARIBBEAN RECORDING CO. LTD.
1 GEFFRARD PLACE, Kingston, Jamaica — Phone 2754 & 33303

Directors: Chairman: Donald Bernard
Managing Director: Deonarine Tewari
Director-Secretary: Leroy S. Riley

Directors: Abe Issa
George Desnoes
Herbert MacDonald
Tony Bridge

Ivan also ran a sound system for hire to play at parties and functions and he played out at stage shows at the Ward Theatre. His influence did not stop here and Chin's Radio Service would prove to be the starting point for the careers of many lifelong music lovers and electronics experts including some notable figures in the history of Jamaican music.

Lloyd 'King Jammy' James' mother obtained his first job for him at Chin's Radio Service and, although Jammy considered that his musical education was with King Tubby, the electronics skills that he was taught at Chin's were invaluable to his career:

"The first amplifier I ever built was while I was at Chin's Radio Service but I didn't get the experience from being at Chin's… I got the experience from being around Tubby's but we had the facilties to build it at Chin's."
King Jammy

Another electronics expert and music lover, Don Gangadeen, reminisced about the time when he worked at Ivan's Church Street shop:

"I worked in the shop from 1958 to 1959 and left in 1960 to come to the UK. I left school and began the 'Learn Radio By Correspondence Course' and then Ivan apprenticed me as a radio engineer. We used to sell emergency lighting units, radios and amplifiers in the shop. Ivan was still doing his calypso thing on the side but we looked on it as old fashioned! We sold a mix of calypso and rhythm & blues in the shops. The country people wanted calypso while the more middle class people would ask for classical.

My big thing was amplifiers. This was the driving force behind my love of music. I wanted to create my own sound but I couldn't afford it so we ordered the chassis and Ivan paid for it. I agreed to pay him back on a weekly basis and I began to build amplifiers for myself. The first was 150 watts using the legendary KT88 valves. Being with Ivan gave me a good background and being the sort of person he was I benefitted tremendously. Today I'm still into music. First thing in the morning I turn on the amplifier. Music helps to create my mood." **Don Gangadeen**

Pat Kelly also served his electronics apprenticeship at Chin's. As well as being one of the best singers Jamaica has ever produced Pat is also a highly accomplished recording engineer who, while not exercising his considerable vocal talents, would go on to work the board at both King Tubby's Studio and Randy's Studio 17.

After leaving Jamaica in 1974 Ivan started Chin's Radio Service in Canada and the family ran four shops "spread out around the city" based in the town of Scarborough in Toronto. Two of his sons ran stores under the Chin's name while another two, Gary and Cliff, operated under their own names. The revival of interest in mento at the beginning of the new Millennium "came as a surprise" to Ivan and, when it was discovered that "Chin's is alive in Toronto", Ivan came out of retirement to "hand make" compact discs of his mento recordings and sell them online. "People only knew about some of the records. Nobody knew that eighty tracks had been recorded". Each set of Chin's CDs (Chin's Calypso Sextet: 'Chin's Calypso Sextet, Kingston Jamaica Volumes One to Five') comes complete with Ivan's certificate stating that the buyers "are the proud owners of original and genuine Chin's CDs and not copies" and a complete history of the Chin's label.

"These CDs bring back things of the past from Jamaica and the words give you a feeling of what was going on in these days. It is hard to believe that those songs were originally recorded with a recorder that used a metal needle to cut grooves into a ten inch disc."   **Ivan Chin**

During the Fifties Ivan Chin's recordings were issued in the UK on the Melodisc subsidiary label Kalypso which was originally an outlet for Trinidadian music. Although this UK based label carried the same name as Ken Khouri's Kalypso label in Jamaica there were no connections between the two.

"Stanley Motta was the man who ran things then Ivan Chin from Chin's Radio down Church Street and then 'Baba' Tewari. The Caribbean Recording Company came next..."   **Bunny 'Striker' Lee**

Deonarine 'Baba'/'Dada' Tewari, an Indian whose family ran Kingston's Regal theatre, opened the Caribbean Recording Company Ltd (CRC) in February 1957 with premises at 118 Orange Street and a small pressing plant at 1 Geffrard Place, Torrington Road, Kingston.

"The Caribbean Recording Company Ltd takes pleasure in announcing their appointment as exclusive pressers, manufacturers and distributors of phonograph records in the British West Indies and British Colonial Africa Regions for the following firms in the United States Of America…"
The Daily Gleaner 11th February 1957

CRC licensed USA masters for manufacture and release in Jamaica and provided pressing facilities at their small plant off Torrington Road. Their impressive list of distributed labels included Imperial, Aladdin, Chess, Checker, Dootone, Duke, Peacock, Specialty, Atlantic, Atco, Modern, Roost and Vee-Jay and artists such as Johnny Ace, Dave Bartholomew, Fats Domino, Ernie Freeman, Roscoe Gordon, Shirley & Lee, Smiley Lewis and Joe Turner.

'The Caribbean Recording Company also began to release mento recordings on their Caribou label. Their mento productions were slightly slicker than those of their contemporaries and included the first commercial recordings of Laurel Aitken and the superb 'Chico Chico' from Count Sticky who was not the same Sticky as the percussionist and foundation deejay, Uzziah Thompson, also known as 'Cool Stick'.

"You have a Sticky named Count Sticky. I know him! He always worked on the North Coast you know… him play the congas but he is a calypso man! He used to live in Pink Lane… I'd go and check him and he'd say 'Hi Sticky' and I'd say 'Hi Sticky!' The two of us used to live nice but we do a different work… totally!" **Uzziah 'Cool Stick' Thompson**

"When CRC started pressing costs came down by 75 per cent… The building was located on Torrington Road almost across from Record Specialists but was later torn down after a fire…"
Kevin O'Brien Chang & Wayne Chen

Some of the earliest Jamaican rhythm & blues recordings were made at 'Baba'/'Dada' Tewari's studio and released through CRC. Percy 'Metro' Miller, a pioneering sound system builder and operator, recalled:

"The first Jamaican original label I remember was Laurel Aitken's 'Aitken's Boogie' on Caribou… it was a 78. Laurel had other things like 'Boogie In My Bones'… he imitated the American singers." **Percy 'Metro' Miller**

"'Baba'/'Dada' Tewari owned the Caribbean Recording Company. He was an Indian man who used to have his own studio too. He made one of the first rhythm & blues tunes in Jamaica with Simms & Robinson (Zoot 'Skully' Simms also known as Mr Foundation & Lloyd 'Bunny' Robinson) but we call them Bunny and Skully. It came out on 78 called 'My Baby Has Left Me'. People don't mention them but they are the backbone of Jamaican music".
Bunny 'Striker' Lee

It is ironic to consider that at exactly the same time that Jamaica was reaching out to the USA for musical inspiration the USA was looking towards the Caribbean for an experience that was perceived to be more 'real' and authentic than their home produced music . In 1945 The Andrews Sisters' cover of Lord Invader's 'Rum & Coca Cola' for Decca sold a reputed seven million copies and started an interest in the USA for all things Caribbean. It is all but forgotten now but the so called 'Calypso Craze' that swept North America in the Fifties sold innumerable records. Films and magazines were produced to satisfy the demands of a public eager to discover more about the music and its performers and Jamaican singer Lord Flea (Norman Thomas) progressed to film appearances after a guest spot on the Perry Como TV show.

"Jamaica did have an international calypso singer... a guy name Lord Flea (sings) 'Where did the naughty little flea go'. He was in some American movies but he died early. He took up the banner and probably, if he was still alive, he would have been as big and as popular as Mighty Sparrow and Lord Kitchener. So those men did a lot for Jamaican music."
Bunny 'Striker' Lee

At the height of the craze Harry Belafonte's 'Calypso' became the first ever album by a solo artist to sell in excess of a million copies "spending thirty one weeks at the top of the US album charts". Harry Belafonte was born in New York to Jamaican parents and "despite the title of the record most of its offerings were, in fact, based on the traditional mento music of Jamaica rather than the calypso of Trinidad".

"From New York he went as a child to Jamaica in the West Indies, the homeland of his parents, where the living was seldom easy and the rhythm and meaning of living was continually expressed in song."
'Belafonte Sings'

"Belafonte is a purist. He argues that all West Indian music is not genuine calypso. He claims that the term has been used much too indiscriminately. 'Two of my big records right now are not even calypso' he charges. 'Jamaica Farewell' is a West Indian folk ballad'…" **Aaron Norman**

There has been considerable confusion amongst musicologists, ethnologists and anthropologists ever since and notions of authenticity and what is 'real' and what is not continue to haunt the music.

"Their rendition of Jamaican folk songs is authentic and should not be confused with popularised versions which have come to be called calypsos, a term which properly applies to a certain type of ballad in Trinidad." **'Authentic Jamaican Folk Songs'**

But the performers, and the record producers, were far more pragmatic:

"If the tourist want calypso that's what we sell them!" **Lord Flea**

Mento was never a music made strictly for the tourists although it was noted that "it is not unreasonable to fear that the demand of the tourist may engender a spurious supply". Mento was local, topical, full of insight and fuelled by an approach that related directly to the Jamaican experience. It had a meaning, a life and a humanity all of its own and mento records were played out nightly on the sound systems in the Fifties.

"When Coxsone first started he used to play mento before he started bringing in the rhythm & blues 78's but we used to call them calypso. Some say **cal**ypso and some say ca**lyp**so." **Bunny 'Striker' Lee**

Duke Reid was one of the first sound system operators to turn his hand to actually producing rather than reproducing music. Although he specialised in playing American rhythm & blues records on his Treasure Isle sound (and on his Treasure Isle Time radio show) the initial 78rpm release on his Trojan label was a recording of the mento standard 'Penny Reel' performed by Lord Power & The Calypso Quintet.

"Duke Reid's first set of tunes was calypso. Lord Power singing 'Penny Reel'…" **Bunny 'Striker' Lee**

Like so many other 'crazes' the 'Calypso Craze' inevitably spluttered to a halt but the Jamaican fascination with American rhythm & blues continued to grow and would eventually lead to the worldwide phenomenon known as reggae. Stanley Motta, Ivan Chin, and 'Baba'/'Dada' Tewari came from widely differing backgrounds but all were driven by a fascination with electronics, recorded sound and an overpowering love of music. These pioneers began to make a reality of recorded music in Jamaica and the business template that they laid down has since been followed by every major record producer in Jamaican music. Mento songs continue to be used as a source of lyrical inspiration and the bombastic names of the performers have been echoed down the years by the hyperbolic titles of innumerable deejays and dance hall stars.

Chin's Radio Services, 48 Church Street, Kingston

Producer, Arranger & Engineer: Ivan Chin

Labels: Chin's, Kalypso

Musicians: **Chin's Calypso Sextet**

"The band that produces the type of records liked by most Jamaicans. Played in homes and on all Sound Systems and Juke Boxes throughout Jamaica."   **Chin's Records 78rpm cover**

Song Composer, Musical Arrangement & Vocals: Alerth Bedasse
Lyrics Composer: Everart Williams
Saxophone: Wilbert Stephenson
Banjo: Cheston Williams
Guitar: Aaron Carr
Bass: Vivian Lord
Maracas: Everart Williams

CRC Caribbean Recording Company Ltd
118 Orange Street, Kingston
& 1 Geffrard Place, off Torrington Road, Kingston

Managing Director: Deonarine 'Baba'/'Dada' Tewari

Labels: Caribou, Down Beat, RCA & Regal

Chapter 3

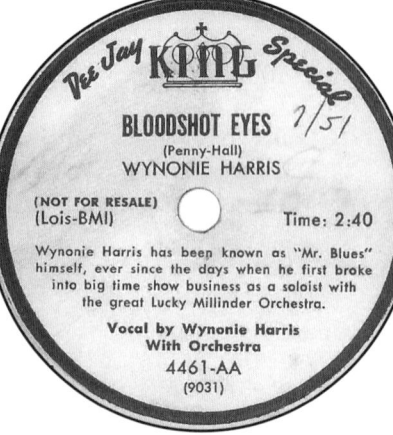

Paul Coote

Chapter 3

Sound Systems Were Like Our Radio Station
RJR & JBC

"Please, Mr Deejay, please play this song for me again…"
'Swing And Dine' The Melodians

"In those early days the only band on the radio was the long wave band and the only thing we could hear was Spanish language stations and Spanish music from Cuba." **Ivan Chin**

The first radio station in Jamaica, VP5PZ, began broadcasting on shortwave in 1939 using equipment belonging to a local business man and 'ham' operator named John Grinan. The initial broadcasts were limited to one hour a week from Mr Grinan's home at 2 Seaview Avenue, St Andrew. Following the outbreak of war in 1939 he donated his equipment to the Jamaican government who, on 1st May 1940, employed a small staff and began broadcasting daily. In addition to news and wartime information, BBC relays and classical music, "live performances of local artistes", were featured on what was now known as ZQI. By 1947 ZQI was broadcasting for four hours a day but the signal could not be heard after dark and it has been estimated that the audience never exceeded 100,000 listeners.

"My earliest musical influences came from the sounds of station ZQI... Billy Eckstine, Nat 'King' Cole, Sarah Vaughan and The Ink Spots and early Jamaican artists Jimmy Tucker... a great singer... Julian Ifla and Edmarine Andrian... that girl could really sing. My uncle, Samuel Powell, performed on the radio too... a great tenor!" **Derrick Harriott**

Radio sets had to have short wave reception in order to pick up BBC broadcasts from England, the Netherlands, Germany and France (which were transmitted on short wave) but sets with a medium wave band could also receive transmissions from Cuba and the Dominican Republic. The signals from some high powered American stations, such as WCKY, WLWO and WLNY, could also be picked up after dark but usually only when prevailing atmospheric conditions facilitated reception.

In 1949 the Jamaican Government granted a licence to the Jamaica Broadcasting Company, a subsidiary of the Rediffusion Group based in London, to operate regular broadcasting and re-diffusion services. Commercial broadcasting began on 9th July 1950 on Radio Jamaica Rediffusion, known as RJR, who had been given a mandate to cover all of Jamaica with radio broadcasting. Wireless receiving sets, or radios, were extremely expensive and very few people could actually afford to own one. Kevin O'Brien Chang & Wayne Chen stated that "in 1950 a modest home hi-fi would set an American back 5% of his annual income. The same set up would cost approximately a whole year's wages for a Jamaican". Inexpensive receivers were not readily available to Jamaica's general public until the introduction of transistor radios in the following decade. Radio sets were distributed to over two hundred designated listening posts throughout the island at places such as village stores, police stations and schools "where people naturally gathered" and by 1956 RJR had a "total average listenership" of about 600,000 people: approximately half the population over the age of nine years.

At this time American rhythm & blues had began to take hold in Jamaica but RJR "programming was heavily middle class and did not reflect popular preferences.... people always complained that Jamaican radio did not play what the public really wanted". RJR certainly did not play the type of music that appealed to the younger generation and those with access to a radio endeavoured to tune in to American radio stations, such as WINZ out of Miami and WNOE out of New Orleans, whose powerful transmitters beamed this brash, boastful music across the Gulf of Mexico out into the

Caribbean. "... and sometimes you would get the station drifting and just hear a tiny snatch of the record. It was on WINZ that I first heard 'Little Bitty Pretty One' by Thurston Harris. We tried all sorts to get a better pick up and less static. Aerials on poles... boosters... everything!"

Percy 'Metro' Miller

In order to cope with the overwhelming demand for rhythm & blues mobile sound systems were established by operators including 'Count Nick The Champ' and Tom Wong who named his sound, 'Tom The Great Sebastian'. This was a tribute to Cornel Wilde's trapeze artist, 'The Great Sebastian' who featured in Cecil B DeMille's film 'The Greatest Show On Earth', Oscar winner for Best Picture of 1952. They became local heroes as they played, promoted and competed to play the latest music to their wildly appreciative and seriously partisan followers on their ever growing sound systems. The original sound systems were basic set ups with one record deck, a valve amplifier and the largest commercially available loudspeakers but they soon became increasingly sophisticated. 'Tom the Great Sebastian' played out with the first amplifier built by the electronics expert Horace Leslie Galbraith as he recalled to Basil Walters.

"From the early Thirties to the Fifties there were exclusive clubs in Kingston with live orchestras, led by George Moxey, Redver Cooke and Mapletoft Poulle amongst others, which were patronised by the St Andrew well to do. For us ordinary people there were no live orchestras but, instead, large homes on Victoria Avenue, Upper King Street and elsewhere, where they hired a radiogram with popular 78rpm records and the patrons paid from two to five shillings entrance fee.

But the music from the scratchy 78rpm records at a radiogram dance was very poor and could only be heard by about twenty people. The sound quality needed to be improved. The music had to be enhanced... less noise, more clarity, 'rounder' bass, voices to be brought out... and more power was needed. Having built the 25 watt amplifiers, I was sure I could build a better amplifier to improve our radiogram dances and set out to do so.

This first, ground breaking model was sold to Tom Wong and was used to start his sound system called 'Tom The Great Sebastian'. Within a few months there were sound system dances all over Kingston at various lodge

Chapter 3

Another top name in the local sound system world V Rocket at the control.

halls, open air lawns and anywhere that could hold a crowd of one hundred people and up. We supplied amplifiers to sound systems all over Kingston and the country parishes. Among the sound systems we supplied amplifiers to were Nick's, Prof, V Rocket, Hoshue, Duke Reid, Coxsone 'Downbeat' Dodd and many others all over Jamaica.

People loved music ... talented people made music ... enterprising individuals got the music recorded and the radio stations and the sound systems took the music to an enthusiastic public. To this day it continues..."
Horace Galbraith

By the latter half of the decade wardrobe sized speaker cabinets known as 'House Of Joy' were commonplace sound system staples ensuring that you felt the music as a physical force rather than merely listened to it. Jo Jo Hookim recalled just how important music was because "it was one of the few forms of entertainment available to the people before television arrived in Jamaica" but he remains sceptical about some of the sound men's claims regarding their exclusive selections.

"In the old days when Coxsone or Duke would announce a record and say 'only me one can play this tune' and everybody would jump up and down and shout 'ray ray ray...' A lot of the time the song wasn't any good anyway. No-one else would have wanted to play the tune!"
Joseph 'Jo Jo' Hoo Kim

The competition between rival sound systems was cut throat, both metaphorically and literally, and their operators' status as Jamaican legends was built on the strength and exclusivity of their selections of American 78rpm records and the size and power of the equipment that they played their discs on. Cecil Bustamente Campbell, known as Prince Buster, in typical boastful style, declaimed to reggae journalist Chris Lane about his Voice Of The People sound system days... although fifty pounds for one record was possibly a slight exaggeration.

"In those days there was a lot of competition. There were often fights at dances and I was always getting my wires cut by people who supported the other sounds. See this scar? A couple of Duke Reid's men came up behind me one night and hit me with a brick because I beat him in a contest. I used to have the best sound then: about five hundred watts with the old 'House Of Joy' horns and speakers. If there was any distortion you would be disqualified in a competition, you know. And I had a good selection of records. That was the trouble you had to have all the best and the latest from the States and sometimes a record by Fats Domino, Amos Milburn or Shirley & Lee would cost as much as fifty pounds!"

Prince Buster

"Sabotage used to go on... they'd go in the dance and get a pin and stick it through the speaker wires and short circuit the sound. All of a sudden the sound started sounding rubbish and you wondered what was going on so they'd go and see... check the wires and see if everything was alright. Then they'd find the pins that the other sound men had stuck in the wires. They'd do so much things... it's unbelievable. They would start fights... that sound man would send his henchmen to your dance if your dance was too nice because he'd want your audience at his dance. So he'd send some bad men in to start a fight and people would run out of the dance then leave and find another dance somewhere else. A whole heap of tricks that they used to use... some of them I wasn't even aware of at the time, you know but looking back I'd say... yeah... these things really used to happen."

Dennis AlCapone

Sound system operators, including Duke Reid 'The Trojan' and Clement 'Sir Coxsone The Downbeat' Dodd, would travel to America on record buying missions and, on their return to Kingston, scratch off all the label details in order to jealously guard the names and the artists of their exclusive finds. The Southern states provided particularly rich pickings: often records they had discovered there would have only been local hits and were consequently unheard of, and unheard, elsewhere. The sound men would then rename the records to further confuse the competition. Coxsone referred to Willis Jackson & His Orchestra's 'Later For The Gator' as 'Coxsone Hop' and 'San Diego Bounce' by Harold Land became 'Downbeat Shuffle' when he played the records exclusively on his Downbeat Sound System. Lesser sounds relied on imported 78's and Lloyd Daley recalled that he obtained many of the records for his Lloyd The Matador sound system from record shops such as Alec Durie's Times Store, 'Savoy' Riley's shop and Jack Taylor's Hardware Store on Orange Street.

"The USA rhythm & blues played by Jamaican sound systems in this period covered a wide range of regional styles which included not only the

oft-cited New Orleans style such as Fats Domino, Professor Longhair and Smiley Lewis but also the Memphis beat of Ike Turner and Rosco Gordon and the Texas shuffles of Clarence 'Gatemouth' Brown, Jimmy McCracklin, and Big Walter along with sides recorded in New York, Chicago, Cincinnati and Los Angeles for labels like Aladdin, Dot, King and Savoy. Balladeers like Billy Eckstine, duos like Gene & Eunice and Shirley & Lee, obscure doo-woppers and vocal groups like The Hawks and The Cliques were popular as were saxophone stylists like Harold Land, Gene Ammons, Maxwell Davis, Sil Austin and Tab Smith. Along with the obvious choices there were plenty that were far more obscure for example Joe Firdy's 'Beck & Call', Felix Cross' 'Cadillac Car' or Charles Saunders' 'Brand New Rocking Chair' which were probably bigger hits in the Jamaican dances than they ever were in their native USA."
Steve Barrow

"The first sound system in Jamaica was Goodie's, then you had a guy named 'Count Nick The Champ', 'Count Jones', 'Smith The Blues Blaster'... all those sounds were before Coxsone and Duke Reid. Every area had their sound. In every district you have a sound. Coxsone used to go to America and do farm work and Duke used to go America so they brought back the American blues records so those men became kings of the arena. But the rhythm & blues tunes were old records... they used to search the record shops for old records... not new tunes. Duke Reid had Cuttings and Coxsone had Count Matchuki (deejays) and when they played these records they'd scratch off the names. Sir Coxsone the Downbeat came from the Downbeat 78 label... but they used to scratch off the titles and give it their own name. Then you had a guy came with a strength of cash from America named 'King Edwards The Giant'. He gave them 'nough trouble! He had a big amplifier named the Hercules that mashed up Coxsone and Duke Reid in 1960, 1961 and 1962... it sent them back to the drawing board and he started his own productions too."
Bunny 'Striker' Lee

"The sound systems started in Kingston but grew rapidly in the rural parts... people would always be very interested in anything that makes a financial return... and the music business was no different. The music grew and lot of people saw this as an opportunity... buying and selling and promotion... it was another way to make a living."
Winston 'Merritone' Blake

"The first one I listened to was Coxsone but at that time Reid was way on top with his records and fans... and his amplification was thousands of watts but we didn't realise that as they were playing in the open air. But if you stood close to their speakers your stomach would move to the power of the music. Each sound system would have its own fans who would travel around with them and each system would try to improve on its records."
Percy 'Metro' Miller

A number of companies began using the radio as a medium of advertisement by sponsoring radio programmes which were either pre-recorded or voiced live from the studio. Duke Reid was one of the first sound system operators to sponsor his own radio show: 'Treasure Isle Time'. Broadcast on a Saturday it initially ran for a quarter of an hour and opened with a cockerel crowing... "It's Treasure Isle Time".

"At that time we were mostly getting foreign songs. We didn't have a radio station and we used to listen to radio from Cuba and all those places but when we started out with our radio station. RJR had a speaker box... no dial or anything just a volume control... so it was only RJR coming through that speaker box and whatever they play is what we know. You just got to listen to it and Jamaica is so musical that even a Japanese dance... that was a hit in Jamaica. We just know music full stop.

But what was played on the radio station was what was paid to be played. They wouldn't play Jamaican music at the time unless, for instance, like Duke Reid who had a slot that he bought on the radio station to promote his music called 'Treasure Isle Time'. It used to start with a Tab Smith tune called 'My Mother's Eyes' but our music wouldn't be played on a regular basis. It was mostly foreign songs we used to hear on the radio... people like Fats Domino, Elvis Presley, Louis Prima, Louis Jordan. All those American music was being played and those were the songs that inspired us... until we started hearing our music that Coxsone and Duke Reid made."
Dennis AlCapone

"Duke was a wealthy man and he'd come back and forwards with any amount of 78's and he'd scrape off the names. So when you hear them say 'It's Treasure Isle Time' on the radio... he was one of the first men to have a record programme. Every Saturday... one in the morning and one

in the evening. His trademark was Tab Smith's 'My Mother's Eyes' then you'd hear 'Treasure Isle Time' for fifteen minutes or half an hour and that became a way of life on the radio 'cause people used to listen out for it."
Bunny 'Striker' Lee

"The music authorities of yesteryear will remember him as Duke Reid The Trojan, King of Sound System (now popularly known as the discotheque) and a pioneer of rhythm & blues in Jamaica. His sound was a household name in music circles in the early Fifties when he popularised rhythm & blues both on his sound system and that well listened Saturday evening radio presentation 'Treasure Isle Time'." **'Greatest Jamaican Beat'**

By 1958 over fifteen thousand subscribers had access to the RJR re-diffusion service which provided "a special service of programmes transmitted by wire. The service was carried to homes, department stores, bars, hotels and police stations and proved very popular". The re-diffusion subscribers were able to receive RJR radio programmes through a loudspeaker but they could only turn the volume up or down or switch the speaker on and off. There were no alternative programmes available.

"RJR was the first station in Jamaica you know ... it name ZQI and when RJR took it over it became Radio Jamaica and then these little re-diffusion things did come in... I think it was from England... and you did rent it from the station and they'd run the wire like how they do the cables now... so every poor man did have a re-diffusion for like eight shillings a month or so with just a little speaker and you'd turn it off or on with a volume on it..." **Bunny 'Striker' Lee**

But from 1958 onwards the tastes of the American audience moved towards an altogether softer, less abrasive sound and the driving rhythm & blues 78rpm discs that had previously been sufficient to ensure a sound system's musical supremacy became increasingly scarce. The top operators realised that, if they wanted to stay ahead of the opposition, they needed to make their own music to play on their sound systems. The more progressive sound system owners began to make one off custom cut discs, known as 'transcription discs', 'reference discs' or 'soft wax' at RJR's one track recording studio originally intending to play these acetates solely on their sets. Not being musicians themselves they turned to the innate musical sensibilities of Kingston's jazz and orchestra band fraternity and men such as Roland Alphonso, Oswald 'Baba' Brooks, Don Drummond, Tommy McCook and

Ernest Ranglin fulfilled their needs. This helped to somewhat soften the blow that the arrival of the sound systems had dealt to many of the island's professional musicians.

"No man. This is what happened when the sound systems started and why the sound system caught on so big. In Jamaica before the sound systems started you used to have orchestra dances but when the orchestra played (at a dance) every second they'd be eating off the promoter's curry goat and drinking his white rum and the promoter wasn't making any money! So when a man started with a little gramophone that he'd brought down to Jamaica and what you now call a PA (public address system) the operator could play twenty four seven and all he had to do was change the needle if it sounded funny! So now the promoters could tell the musicians to take your instruments and go… and you used to have places like Coney Island on East Queen Street where they played out every night."   **Bunny 'Striker' Lee**

"My concern about sound systems is they played all the music but they have... I don't know... in a way they competed with the bands. I remember 'Soul Shot', which was a popular sound system, was due to play in a night club to replace a band that wasn't there because the band was travelling and they started to take over because it was easier and cheaper for the club to use a sound system. You only have one or two people to look after but when you had a band you had eight or ten people so it was less expensive. But when the live bands started to travel overseas then you had to replace them with sound systems..."   **Ronnie Nasralla**

"We played all over St. Thomas and people started to hear about us in Kingston. We had connections in Kingston but sound systems were looked down on as degrading places to be. It was the era of orchestra dances but we used to play American rhythm & blues records like Fats Domino's 'Going To The River' and Smiley Lewis' 'I Hear You Knocking'. The crowd would dance 'The Yank' which was a hip jerking dance and if danced enthusiastically it could cause dislocated hips! There was headline in the paper 'No room in the hospital for Yankers!'"
Winston 'Merritone' Blake

"We used to listen to the local juke boxes and American rhythm & blues shows on the radio but would also go to listen to the top sound systems playing out such as Duke Reid, Sir Coxsone and King Edwards. But we weren't allowed in because we were too young so we had to stop outside and make sure we reached home by nine o'clock! We used to sit on the car tops on Upper Waltham Avenue and I would sing pitching between Owen Gray and Derrick Morgan to try and develop something for myself. I did one song called 'She's Mine' for King Edwards The Giant down on Spanish Town Road. He was a top producer and I was just glad to be included with artists such as Delroy Wilson, The Maytals and all them guys."

Winston 'Groovy' Tucker

This 'local' music proved so popular, and the demand so great, that the operators began to release it commercially and became record producers. Coxsone Dodd, Duke Reid and Prince Buster were among the first to establish themselves in this new role and their influence was to prove profound. However, not all of the sound men made this all important transition.

"Because when the rhythm & blues thing started to dry up every sound man started to make his own records so there's a lot of sound men who have tunes that never came out. But you had a lot of producers at that time. One of the first producers was a man called Smithy. He was a customs broker and he had a record shop where he used to sell a lot of the American rhythm & blues records. (Bunny is referring to Simeon L Smith's Hi-Lite Music Store at 163 Spanish Town Road, Kingston 13 who released his own productions on the Smiths, Faith, Hi-Lite and Hero labels).

At that time the top artists in Jamaica were Rosco Gordon, Louis Armstrong and Louis Jordan. Louis Jordan was like the king! Smiley Lewis, Fats Domino... When those records came out that was in the 78 days until the format changed to 45 and seven inch... When we used to get a 78 cut (to play on the sound) we used to call it a 'soft wax'. Now they call it dub."

Bunny 'Striker' Lee

These early Jamaican recordings have been criticised because of their alleged raw raucousness but there is a sophistication and a subtlety, coupled with an underlying rhythmic complexity, to the music that is too often overlooked. These records were far more than straightforward copies that vainly attempted to capture the spirit and feel of American rhythm & blues. They were unmistakeably Jamaican in form and content and a sound was gradually created that was not only totally new and original but that would go on to outlive many of its influences. This authentic new music combined the driving drum and bass beat derived from rhythm & blues and boogie woogie from the USA, the influences of the big bands of Stan Kenton and Duke Ellington, Forties swing bands and free blowing be-bop; South American Latin influences blended together with African based buru drumming, the religious fervour and drumming techniques of pocomania (which combined Christian and African religious elements), jonkanoo (a West African fertility ritual) and Rastafarian ideology; quadrille's formality, mento's topicality and local 'story telling' lyrics. Sound system deejays including Michael 'Count Matchuki' Cooper, Winston 'King Stitt' Sparkes, Uzziah 'Cool Stick' Thompson, Percy 'Sir Lord Comic' Wauchope & Noel 'King Sporty' Williams all developed their own highly individual 'jive talking' introductions learnt from American radio deejays and later local hero Canadian Charlie Babcock "the Cool Fool with the Live Jive!" on RJR.

"I used to lift sound box, House of Joy, and all those things for Coxsone and for Duke Reid… until we started to play… put on records and deejay. I do songs for Coxsone named 'Guns Of Navarone', 'Ball A Fire' all them tune there! A song for Duke Reid named 'Guns Fever'. I deejayed on Coxsone, Duke Reid, Count Boysie. Coxsone come hear me one day a deejay and take me go a studio one time and just said 'do the same thing'. I didn't know my rights… I didn't know nothing! But the song came out and did nice and me get a little something. Give thanks still but those songs weren't my personal thing… yes… but you know me no get no title nor credit nor little nothing. But me no fussy still… that's what me a show you… me just cool. Me will get my own when it comes…" **Uzziah 'Cool Stick' Thompson**

Film and television themes, sentimental ballads, country & western songs, gospel harmonising and nursery rhymes were all mixed up, mixed down and blended together into one seamless whole. The rhythmic emphasis was placed firmly on the offbeat and at some point between 1961 and 1962, exactly when it is impossible to say, Jamaican rhythm & blues or shuffle and boogie developed into ska and a completely new genre was born. Kingston's entrepreneurs continued to exploit a seemingly unstoppable and endless wealth of local vocal and instrumental talent.

"The beat in ska is a pocomania beat and the music moves with the seasons. It's in time with nature." **Prince Buster**

The majority of these early recordings were made illicitly at RJR under the direction of one of the key figures in the development of the Jamaican recording industry: a young Australian named Graeme Goodall. Born in Melbourne in 1932 he gained his first experience in Australia in the early Fifties making field recordings of "things like square dance bands, multi-voice choirs". He then moved to the UK where he worked for a company called Universal Programme Corporation based in central London in Portland Place close to the BBC headquarters. UPC made programmes for Radio Luxembourg. At that time Radio Luxembourg was the only station in the UK where you could hear nightly pop music programmes but it was broadcast at night time only and the signal would keep drifting and fading, drifting and fading.

"Well I was born in Melbourne, Australia in 1932. I went to Scotch College in Melbourne and I wanted to be a marine radio operator but part of that was that I had to go to college so I went to Melbourne Technical College, which is now the Royal Melbourne Institute of Technology, and to support myself I got a job in a radio station... broadcasting.

Right, there's 3KZ in Melbourne and of course, as I say, being a shift kicker, I got all the jobs that nobody else wanted and part of that was going out and doing live broadcast with big bands, square-dancing bands, things like that, and so I went out I did that. My formal music training, was believe it or not, as a boy at school, you know as a singer, but at fourteen of course the voice goes and so did my musical training. But of course at one time there I was working in a record library, pulling records, and so this latent interest and love of music just sort of blossomed. So around about 1954 I decided all the engineers in broadcasting seemed to be very young and very healthy and I was probably going to die before I would be promoted so, with that in mind, I thought 'Well there's this thing called television on the horizon so why don't I go and learn that?' Well I can go to two places to learn that: one is the United Kingdom where all they had was the BBC in those days or the other alternative is to go to the United States of America. But the US in those days, unlike President Bush's new thing where if you can get across the Rio Grande you can get a job, in those days you had to support yourself and you weren't allowed to work. So that sort of ruled that out. So I remember paying £76.00 sterling, getting on the P&O Orient liner in Melbourne, staying in a cabin sleeping six below the waterline and went to England. And when I got to England, again luckily enough, I got a job with UPC... the

Universal Programme Corporation... in Portland Place. And even though I was taken on to do recorded programmes, like 'Shilling A Second', 'People Are Funny' and 'Strike It Rich' these radio shows for Radio Luxembourg, part of it was supported by themselves by doing independent recording. Petula Clark was amongst them I remember and 'Little Shoemaker' was just one of my things. I was a tape operator, operating these big EMI tape machines, and my job was to press these buttons and let the geniuses do the recording but I learnt a lot about it in the process while I was there."

Graeme Goodall

While working at UPC Graeme was advised to go to Rediffusion who "were looking for engineers to go into the Overseas Division" and in late 1954 he moved to Jamaica, initially on a three year contract, to install "this new FM service" at Radio Jamaica.

"While I was at UPC I met a person they introduced me to, RP Gabriel, whose son, Peter, later on became famous in music of course. RP Gabriel was the director of engineering for Rediffusion, Overseas Rediffusion Services, and of course commercial radio people were something of a nonentity in Britain as you can well imagine. He gave me a job and said 'OK we're sending you to Jamaica'. Well it wasn't as easy as that as he said, 'You can either go to Jamaica or Nigeria' and frankly I didn't know where the hell either of them was so I remember coming out of Carlton House in Lower Regent Street walking across to BOAC and saying 'Have you got any brochures on Nigeria or Jamaica?' And they looked at me askance and they said 'Well we don't have anything on Nigeria but we do have this one on Jamaica' and there were palm trees and ladies walking along with bundles on their heads and dusky maidens all around so I said 'That's for me!' So I went to Jamaica working for Radio Jamaica... and so I went there and again got involved a lot in the music thing but not formally as such. We did a lot of live talent parades. On one of them I met and became firm friends with for many, many years, until he died in fact, was Roland Alphonso. He was a boy of about eighteen. I wasn't much older myself and we became firm friends doing the Colgate Palmolive Talent Parade. That was I guess in 1955 through 1956.

Radio Jamaica (RJR) was owned by Rediffusion which piped RJR programmes all over Kingston and St. Andrew by means of a cable... I had crews of seventy line men... it was a 'wired' network used to send audio signal round on a seventy volt lines and they used to have a speaker that they hung on the wall with a volume control for which they charged the public seven shillings a month. For one programme! We had two and a half kilo watt audio amplifiers, tube amplifiers, so anyway at the end of 1957 I went back to Australia on, as they called it, 'overseas leave'. And when I was there in Australia, I actually took an extended one, like six months, working for GTV, Channel 9 in Melbourne, television, and again the whole thing came up that who was there, who had an engineering background, engineering knowledge and could mix live music. So guess who?

So I worked at Channel 9 and so I got a bit bored. All my friends had grown up... were all married and had children and their wives certainly didn't want to have this rambunctious bachelor wearing American clothes wandering around taking their husbands astray. So I went back to Jamaica."
Graeme Goodall

On his return Graeme signed for another term and also became involved with starting up the new government backed station, JBC, "putting up antennas for them" and making recordings of "live band stuff" in their "large concert studio". When the Jamaican Government decided to introduce its own public broadcasting station, the Jamaican Broadcasting Corporation, the name of RJR was formally changed to Radio Jamaica Limited although it would continue to be known as RJR for many years to come.

The Jamaica Broadcasting Corporation (JBC) was founded by Prime Minster Norman Manley in 1959 as a public broadcasting company using the BBC, and other national broadcasting companies, as its template. It was established in December 1958 by legislation as a "state owned and statutory corporation" and went on air on 15th June 1959. It initially aimed to provide a greater focus on Jamaican culture with a drama department producing original programmes and a resident big band that included Sonny Bradshaw and Ernest Ranglin.

"The Jamaica Broadcasting Corporation organisation was the brainchild of Norman Manley who was premier at the time. He had long felt that Radio Jamaica, which was owned by a big British conglomerate with stations strewn across the empire, was not doing a good enough job in developing a national culture and character."
Keeble McFarlane

A change in government following independence in 1962 led to accusations of political bias of its journalists for allegedly championing Norman Manley's People's National Party (PNP) government. Two years later this resulted in one of the longest ever strikes in Jamaican history following which the majority of the original news journalists lost their jobs and "many talented broadcasters from the presentation, production, technical and clerical side of the business left the country".

"At one time you only had that one radio station in Jamaica RJR (Radio Jamaica Rediffusion) and the parent company was somewhere in England... then JBC came from the government." **Bunny 'Striker' Lee**

"Anyway so it went from there and my term was up at Radio Jamaica and, after putting in at JBC (Jamaican Broadcasting Corporation), we built their transmitters for them, shared facilities, shared transmitter sites. So I was involved in that. Establishing the FM links through the island but the music was the love while the engineering was paying the bills. Mind you, I loved the engineering side of it too. However, I was not an RF (Radio Frequency) man. Deep down I was an audio man." **Graeme Goodall**

Graeme Goodall soon established a considerable reputation through his knowledge of the recording business. He was approached by Chris Blackwell who, at the time, was operating some Wurlitzer juke boxes that "he had obtained from a man named John Elliot" but was growing increasingly frustrated with having to travel to Miami to obtain records to play in them. Chris Blackwell soon came to the same conclusion that Stanley Motta and Ivan Chin had reached earlier in the decade: "these people are playing in bands in hotels... I've got to make records of them so I can sell them to the tourists".

"That was I guess in 1955 through 1956. The only recording that was done in those days was by Motta's Recording, which was Motta's Recording Studio. Stanley Motta had a dealership for radio and electronics and somehow or other he managed to hack together a disc recorder with I think, at best two microphones, and a room which was draped with carpets and anything else he could find and that was the only recording so...

That was in Harbour Street I believe, behind his radio store. I knew Stanley very well and you know quite frankly I just had an interest in the radio, so I started working for Radio Jamaica... well Jamaica Broadcasting Company... as it was in those days.

And in the meantime, well, I met a young lady there and she was being pursued rather heavily by a young man by the name of Chris Blackwell. And at the same time some three or four musicians came from Australia to work in a nightclub over there. A place called the Glass Bucket. One of them was Dennis Sindrey, the pianist was Peter Stoddart and the drummer was Lowell Morris. The clarinettist I forget but anyway he eventually left but, to cut a long story short, eventually I met Chris at a wedding and we got to talking. He said that he wanted to make records and he'd heard that I was the person who knew something about it, and I remember full well that I was so intrigued. I was half drunk at the time too! I sent this young lady home and told her to go packing because I had business to talk and eventually, three years later, I ended up marrying her...my wife Fay. And we've been married for forty years.

So, anyway, Chris got together with Dennis Sindrey and we started making records maybe because Chris Blackwell had somehow or other talked himself into renting six juke boxes from a friend of his. His friend had an outboard motor dealership, and he also had the concession for the juke boxes but he didn't really know what to do with them. So Chris took these on and Chris being Chris said 'Why am I buying records? Why don't I make them myself?'

This is how it started and strangely enough that was fine but he had nowhere to record so I used to go into Radio Jamaica studios after they shut down at night because the band that he was using, including Dennis Sindrey and Peter and all the other guys like Lloyd Brevett, they were all working nightclubs. So they'd close off the gig in the nightclub then rush back to the studios of Radio Jamaica where we'd make records till five o'clock in the morning. And I was taking equipment out of the outside broadcast van to supplement the rather limited equipment we had in the studios. And so I was supplementing that acoustically greatly. Of course, I was limited in the amount of inputs in the mixer and everything and it was sort of... basic."

Graeme Goodall

The RJR studio's one track recording facilities could only be used at night when the radio station was "virtually closed down". Kingston's best musicians were all playing in the nightclubs and hotels so recording could not start until after midnight and would continue to "the wee small hours of the morning". At first the sound was not sufficiently animated and Graeme set up "the first echo chamber ever in the West Indies" by using "all the outside broadcast remote gear... in the men's washroom." Graeme recounted:

"I will be only too happy to describe to you my reasoning/experimenting with recording early Jamaican music. I was born in Caulfield and started off at 3KZ Melbourne Firstly, I, and the 'core' of The Caribs, were all displaced Aussies living in Jamaica. The Caribs were Dennis Sindrey on guitar & vocals from Camberwell; Peter Stoddart on piano from South Australia and Lowell Morris on drums from South Melbourne.

The early pop music of Jamaica, Owen Gray, Laurel Aitken, Keith & Enid, Wilfred Edwards were produced by Chris Blackwell and backed by the Caribs. We used the studios of Radio Jamaica, where I was ACE, after hours....the Caribs were working at the Myrtle Bank Hotel 'til midnight. I borrowed a lot of extra equipment from Radio Jamaica's remote van and used the men's dunnee (washroom/toilet) as a live echo chamber."
Graeme Goodall

"I remember showing Dennis Sindrey how to direct inject a guitar into the mixer and tweak them all out and I got that great top end sound of guitars. Dennis had a Fender twin reverb which he used to sleep with! He put under his bed at night. He was so proud of that but, anyway, I needed an echo chamber and I remember bringing from home a Grundig radio that was owned by Radio Jamaica that we used to monitor the stations and I used to bring that down and put it in the men's restroom then put a microphone up in the centre of the restroom and use it as an echo chamber which worked very, very well...until the night-watchman decided to use the restroom one night in the middle of a take! He walked in and flushed the toilet which spoiled an otherwise good take." **Graeme Goodall**

Although the music was being made at the radio stations the late night comings and goings of the sound system operators, the record producers and their ad hoc groups of musicians did not impinge on either of Kingston's radio stations' agenda. It did not mean that the music would get airplay and both radio stations maintained an ambivalent attitude throughout the entire era of Jamaican music's greatest invention and innovation. RJR and JBC would continue to largely ignore Jamaican music, although some small concessions were made, including the introduction of weekly charts for the best selling records. The first JBC charts came out in August 1959 and, the following month, Laurel Aitken's 'Boogie Rock' on the Caribbean Recording Company's Down Beat label became the first local record to make it on to the chart.

"Dad (Ken Khouri) fought for an interest, fought politically to get recognition for the artists and to get their records played on the radio… out of anything else that was one of the most important things he did. This was in the calypso, mento, pocomania days. The music wasn't recognised by the radio stations but now the radio stations play 99% Jamaican music. He didn't get the recognition for that because he wasn't out there selling his name. We weren't born for that…" **Paul Khouri**

Chris Blackwell and Graeme Goodall began to regularly record local artists in the RJR studio for Chris Blackwell's Island label, named after either Alec Waugh's Fifties novel 'Island In The Sun' or Harry Belafonte's Fifties recording of the same name. Island released ballads including Wilfred 'Jackie' Edwards' 'Whenever There's Moonlight', Owen Grey with 'The Plea' on the R&B label and straight ahead rhythm & blues with Laurel Aitken, whose 'Boogie In My Bones'/'Little Sheila', was issued, naturally, enough on the R&B label. Both sides of this release became the first Jamaican Number One records on the JBC charts.

Many other producers, including Vincent 'Randy's' Chin and Prince Buster, recorded hits at the RJR studios. 'Rico Special' released on Randy's by Rico Rodriguez under the direction of Keith 'Sticky' Parks and Prince Buster's 'Thirty Pieces Of Silver' released on his Voice Of The People label and engineered by Lynford 'Andy Capp' Anderson were both made at Lyndhurst Road.

"'Sticky' Parks? He was a great engineer too at RJR. He was Coxsone's right hand man but when he went to America other people stepped in like Al Plummer… Al was the main studio engineer. He used to schedule the work for the rest of them. He just retired the other day… the longest serving engineer to serve at RJR. Lynford 'Andy Capp' Anderson was an engineer at the radio station. Andy Capp was a very creative engineer. First of all he used to work at RJR studio…" **Bunny 'Striker' Lee**

"That's right… that is correct. Some of my father's (Vincent 'Randy's' Chin) recordings were done at the radio station, what was at RJR… Radio One, under the engineering flagship of a man by the name of Keith 'Sticky' Parks that recorded 'Rico Special'. And these are all factual things I'm telling you, because I was present. The first time I've ever been to a radio station that had one mic, an RCA mic, to capture the sounds." **Clive Chin**

Many other hits were made at JBC's two track recording facilities. The Skatalites recorded one of their now legendary sessions for Justin 'Philip' Yap's Top Deck Records in the JBC Half Way Tree studios. 'Oh Carolina', a massive breakthrough record from the Folks Brothers featuring the Count Ossie Afro Combo and the first to feature Nyahbinghi style drumming, was also recorded at the JBC studios for Prince Buster who released it on his Buster Wild Bells label. Although this music was being made primarily by the sound system operators for the sound system followers the record producers now began to fight hard to get their records played on the radio. Airplay invariably meant that a tune would "take on" because "the people buy what they hear on the radio".

"And the greatest way to sell records is through the radio…."
Dennis AlCapone

"RJR didn't play Jamaican music… they played mostly English music. When JBC came on they started to have much more… Miss Lou and Ranny Williams. There was a live show 'Teenage Dance Party' that was extremely popular broadcast from The Glass Bucket Club (later The VIP Club). All the young people would listen, you could get passes, meet all the artists of the day… it was an extremely popular show."
Winston 'Merritone' Blake

The legendary Bunny 'Striker' Lee first started in the music business promoting records on the radio… by any means necessary. He recounts numerous amusing stories about how he managed to get records played on JBC's 'Teenage Dance Party', a 'record request' programme, produced by jazz musician Sonny Bradshaw. The show originally played only American rhythm & blues but it now began to include local tunes and it was one of the few radio programmes, away from the sponsored shows, to feature Jamaican music.

"I used to like dancing and I used to go with my friends to a thing named 'Teenage Dance Party' at JBC and the programme became very popular... in those days you used to have a panel that 'phoned in to say whether the tune was a hit or a miss. For instance you'd call me and say you want this tune to get power play and your tune got power play if it was voted a hit by the panel. Then it would play every day (on the radio) so then the people were hearing it and they'd get to like it and buy it. Even if the tunes were garbage the people would hear it, get brainwashed and they'd buy it! Yeah man!

That's why we used get records from Duke Reid, Coxsone, King Edwards then Joe Gibbs, Ken Lack and all those other people and promote them ... and we'd go out on a Saturday night promoting the records.

I had an announcer friend who used to work on a Saturday night and we'd go to the front desk at RJR and JBC and call the deejays. We'd claim that we were calling from Montego Bay and Port Royal and Negril and all those places but we'd be calling right from RJR's or JBC's front desk! And not the one voice because the people would get wise so we'd have a set of girls and guys with us. I had the two stations locked!

So the tune played all twenty times on a Saturday night: ten times on RJR and ten times on JBC and on Monday morning everyone would be in the shops asking for it so... Yes! So that was one way of plugging a record..."

Bunny 'Striker' Lee

Towards the end of the decade when Striker became a successful record producer he was able to use more legitimate methods.

"'Cause the people buy what they hear on the radio so I started a programme named 'The Bunny Lee Show' every Thursday night before the people came from in the country on Friday to buy up their stocks. Same time on the two radio stations! Vincent Chin from Randy's... they're VP now... used to sponsor me so it was 'The Bunny Lee Show From Randy's A Go Go'. He used to pay half of the money and I had to find the other half. At the time fifteen minutes on the radio would cost $12,000 so it was quite expensive but the advertisement paid off. So I started off with 'Bunny Lee From Randy's A Go Go' right? So I advertised both Randy's business and mine until later on I went on my own with 'The Bunny Lee Show' at eleven o'clock on Thursday night and I arranged it with both radio stations that any of the two radio stations you tuned into you'd hear 'The Bunny Lee Show'! So you couldn't miss it! People used to say 'Bunny Lee you're mad man! Your radio show starts when everybody's gone to bed!' but when they discovered I was getting results Coxsone and everybody started! You understand? I gradually worked up from fifteen minutes to half an hour. On Friday the country people come in to town to buy their records and the shop was full, or they'd go to Randy's or a next big shop named KG's. So everybody discovered that advertising brought results… and everybody started their show." **Bunny 'Striker' Lee**

Coxsone's radio show was called 'The Sound Of Young Jamaica' and Lee 'Scratch' Perry later sponsored 'The Upsetter Radio Show' on JBC but many of the younger producers were unable to compete with these successful entrepreneurs. When Jimmy Radway established his own label in 1972 he named it 'Fe Me Time' in a direct challenge to the sponsored radio shows.

"I got the idea from the radio when the radio jocks would say 'Lee Perry Time' or 'Bunny Lee Time' and I was constantly being told it's not your time yet. I was tired to hear about that man's time…" **Jimmy Radway**

The debut release on Fe Me Time, 'Black Cinderella' by Errol Dunkley with the label printed by "Lloyd at the corner of Orange Street and North Street", was a resounding Number One hit on both RJR and JBC radio stations in Jamaica but Jimmy insisted "Trust me! I never pay a cent in payola".

Throughout the Sixties and Seventies record producers and artists grumbled constantly about the absence of airplay away from the sponsored shows and also complained bitterly about other producers' records being treated more favourably than the releases on their labels.

"Mrs Pottinger put out some big hit tunes for me too! They were my tunes but through Mrs Pottinger could get radio play… when you wanted to break an artist you gave Mrs Pottinger the tune. It wasn't about money but getting the artist to break because, once they had the hit, they get a name and the stage shows are going to come…

You see those were the days there were too much records for one man to put out. You don't want to look greedy and the radio stations will only play one. If they play one on Lee's they're not going to play one on Jackpot so you might have six different records with six different labels… Six different records and you don't put your name on it as the producer until it's a hit!

One time I had a John Holt tune that I put on Federal Records so that it would get radio play and when the tune became a hit the company demanded to know: 'What is John Holt doing on Federal?' And when they found out it was mine I said 'Well call the police!' They wanted to know how I got the label and put it on my record to get the plays! But they were getting the play and we can't get the play…

Byron Lee would come out with something and you'd hear it twenty four seven across the board. Mrs Pottinger came with the same thing. You understand? Whether their tunes were good or not they would hit! So the sound system was our vibes…" **Bunny 'Striker' Lee**

"The radio stations don't always play your records. One plays reasonably. The other one will just throw your records in the dustbin!"
Augustus 'Gussie' Clarke

"Those do-overs (of Little Roy's 'Tribal War' by John Holt for Channel One and George Nooks for Joe Gibbs) prove I never get any justice with my one! The radio deejays never give me no play but the song hit on its own. The other versions got a lot more play but my one sold as much or more. It was the fastest selling song in the record shops but it didn't show on the chart." **Earl 'Little Roy' Lowe**

"The radio stations had their preferred labels and songs but when we played a record the radio stations had to play it… 'Give the record to Merritone, man!' After playing it for days I would introduce the record and sometimes it would become a hit record!" **Winston 'Merritone' Blake**

But even if the radio was not going to give fair play to their releases it was not going to stop the producers from making music. Their records were played incessantly on the island's juke boxes and sound systems and on sounds in the UK, Canada and America run by expatriate Jamaicans. Many of the records would only ever be heard on the sound systems.

"Tubbys was mashing up the place and from Tubbys played your song the whole place mashed down! Everybody went to dances then and you didn't hear these tunes on the radio." **Linval Thompson**

"'Cause sound system popularise all the records. The radio station don't play no record until them hear somebody a talk about it… or unless you bribe them." **Osbourne 'King Tubby' Ruddock**

"In the immigrant areas of Britain's cities sounds… were the equivalent of an underground radio network." **Steve Barrow & Peter Dalton**

Leonard 'Santic' Chin recalled, if a little elliptically, how 'Pablo In Dub' by Augustus Pablo, a record which helped to establish Leonard's Santic Records, came to be featured as background music on the 'Dulcimena' show. Leonard recalled that it was practically unheard of at that time to hear a "Jamaican produced 'local' instrumental record over the airwaves" but he appreciated that "the piper have to be paid".

"'Cause as good as a tune is and it will play in the dance halls radio play will get it to a different level. There are a lot of people who don't go to the dance halls. There wasn't much reggae played on the radio… I used to think how come all these foreign records get so much play? Every programme, every deejay used to play them and I'd think what happened to all the good Jamaican reggae tunes that were out there?

But when I started recording I soon realised that the system wasn't really as it seemed. You were told to drop your records off at the station and they'd get played… but that wasn't how it really went. You had to know somebody. You had to have a friend. You had to have a man who's looking after your business at the station… and that's how you're going to get some play. And I had my friends at the radio station… sometimes you have to reach out to people… it depends on what you want. I was cool because I knew the rules. From I was a youth I always understood there was nothing for nothing. You don't get things for nothing… the piper have to be paid! I believe that… because if you can do something to help what I'm doing and I have to do that… as long as it's reasonable enough.

When 'Pablo In Dub' started getting radio play everyone said 'How come they're playing this? It's an instrumental record'. At that time the radio would only play vocal records. They would hardly ever play deejay records either... Big Youth's 'S90 Skank' was one notable exception. There was a radio programme called 'Dulcimena'... which was a talk show... and one Saturday night right through it was 'Pablo In Dub' playing in the background. On the juke box... in the bar... it was all 'Pablo In Dub'! I thought to myself it was weird hearing my production on this programme that everybody listened to.

So the big men out there were asking 'What is going down?' I remember one day I was in Randy's shop... everybody in the business used to congregate at Randy's anyway... and everybody knew who I was by then. Someone said to me 'Who is your friend at the radio station?' and I laughed and said 'What do you mean?' and they said 'Come on Chin... nobody's tunes get played the way your tune's getting played. You must have a good friend!' I said 'Not really. Basically I just carry the records to the station like RJR, drop them there and... talk to them nice and ask them to give the records a few plays for me. Because I'd get to understand that if a record is played on the radio then the people will want it... and they said 'Chin! You know that's not the way it goes!'" **Leonard 'Santic' Chin**

"You'd just go 'pon a man's rhythm... 'Pablo just help him out'. Santic... I really did help him out! I never really liked 'Pablo In Dub' you know... at the time it just grew on the people them and there was a connection with the radio station. The music kinda reached the radio station man and they never stopped working on it until it got to Number One... on the two stations! Yeah man!" **Augustus Pablo**

But, away from the sponsored shows, the amount of 'local' records played on the island's two stations was minimal while pop, soul and country & western music ruled the airwaves. Singer and deejay, Dave Barker who would go on to top the UK charts in March 1971 with 'Double Barrel' as one half of 'Dave and Ansel Collins', recalled the continuing influence of American radio stations and records.

"At a very young age I can remember... we used to live in a big tenement yard and you find a few people in the yard who could afford a radio: big ones with a light on the front. We listened to WINZ from the States. There was a lot of rhythm and blues before the soul came out. I didn't go out but some local sound men just string up them sound on the street at St Albans

Lane. I can't remember their names. They were just local men from the yards who had their own sound but never really played out as such. Mostly soul was played. I was about twelve and to me, at that time, the American stuff was rich and superb. All of them soul music: James Brown, Wilson Pickett, Chuck Jackson, Garnett Mimms, Jerry Butler and Gene Chandler. It was fun listening to them songs. It lifted me up and I found myself singing just like them! To me the Jamaican artists sounded extremely good and it made me want to start recording but they never hit me like the soul stuff. There was more emotion in the soul stuff. However Owen Gray did a song that really, really caught me... 'Millie Girl'." **Dave Barker**

The undercurrent of rumours of producers and artists paying or providing favours to the radio deejays to play their records, popularly referred to as payola, were never far from the surface and, occasionally, a full blown scandal would erupt when names would be named.

"I refused to pay the payola because they wanted too much money. You used to have guy named Radcliffe Butler and some other people... Radcliffe Butler and a young announcer they were in the scandal. I broke that scandal in the late Sixties, you know, at JBC. They fired him. If you want your tune to go in the chart and you pay you get plays. After that I became a marked man and they wouldn't play my music... that's why I had to play it on the sound systems like Merritone and come to England." **Bunny 'Striker' Lee**

Derrick Harriott recalled Striker's time as a "marked man" when the radio stations refused to play Bunny Lee productions and, in particular, 'Watch This Sound' by The Uniques but Derrick was having none of it.

"Everybody lived good. We were very close... so close that when the payola thing bust in 1968 all the disc jockeys decided that they would not play the Bunny Lee song, 'Watch This Sound' by The Uniques but I played it on 'The Derrick Harriott Show' on RJR. Man couldn't stop me and Bunny had to come back!" **Derrick Harriott**

A report from the late Sixties in the *The Daily Gleaner's* 'Merry Go Round' column not only mentioned a short lived 'pirate' radio station in Kingston but also encapsulated the then current state of radio programming in Jamaica. It is worth quoting in full despite the author's dismissive attitude towards records that are now considered to be all time classics of the reggae genre such as King Stitt's 'The Ugly One', also known as 'Lee Van Cleef', and Andy Capp's 'Pop A Top'.

"Pirate radio Jamaica recently came to Jamaica... but could be unplugged imminently by the police for operating without a licence. On and off, mainly on Wednesdays and Sundays around midnight, the Allman Town located 'radio station' pumps out reggae through a veil of distortion and interference. The operators are alleged to have connections with local record producers and even broadcast 'commercials' for well known Kingston record shops. It's on the dial at about 11.50 but is so weak by the time you've reached Cross Roads it can't be heard.

Undoubtedly this won't be the last attempt to bring pirate radio to the island. Speculation that a station could be set up in the Cayman Islands to beam to Jamaica is not unrealistic particularly if, as it has been rumoured, the Jamaican Government turned down a recent bid to start a third station by a group of record producers. Of course, the phenomenon of Radio Allman Town underlines two facts of commercial life. The first is that both RJR and JBC have limited airtime left for sponsored radio programmes; the second fact is that the competition between local record producers is fiercer than ever. No doubt the broadcasting authorities have some ideas about alleviating the airtime squeeze but what will happen on the recording scene should be sheer fireworks.

The two dozen leading independent producers (those that have no franchises for overseas labels) continue to spread payola amongst some disc jockeys via rent, hire purchase payments and sundry gifts. This makes itself apparent in the selections played on the air and the ratings received on each station's hit parade.

Both stations are planning renewed attacks on the problem of lifting the standard of music being scheduled. JBC Programme Director, Noel Gayle, says specifically that the station has a responsibility for dictating taste in music. This doesn't preclude reggae at all... it just eliminates the substantial quantity of artistically and technically substandard material that is around.

The rewards for clicking with a hit reggae in Jamaica are lucrative and can generate sales in Britain, Canada and even in the USA yet the expense of production is still relatively low so even the most inexperienced can try to break into the magic circle. But with limited opportunity to have his record broadcast a producer is hard put to get the exposure that his tune needs. His pressure undoubtedly influences 'official' hit parade ratings as can be seen from the fact that the top tunes on RJR and JBC vary considerably. Each station claims its own 'true, accurate and unbiased account' of record popularity: based primarily on retail sales reports, juke box plays, discotheques and requests. Neither apparently can claim to provide an accurate national rating. However both stations are anxious to devise a more reliable system of ranking the hit parade in an effort to stem mounting criticism from the disc manufacturers. The latter point to the USA where the two entertainment trade publications, Cash Box and Billboard, independently produce weekly ratings which, more often than not, show similar results...

On their side the manufacturers would like to see a more authentic hit parade calculated each week. They claim not to participate in the payola system and lately have been investing heavily in sponsored radio programmes to get their foreign franchise records played.

Another odd fact about the recording industry is that many best sellers get little or no exposure on Jamaican radio. The 'blue' records like 'Wreck A Pum Pum' never get past the juke box stage and even the more innocuous erotic sounds such as 'Je T' aime... Moi Non Plus' experience mixed fortunes (banned two weeks ago it's being played again on radio subject to complaints from a little old lady in Brown's Town). Contemporary movie violence featured on a 'local' reggae entitled 'Lee Van Cleef' thankfully got the thumbs down for its "Kill... Kill... Kill..." lyrics (sic). More melodic but equally controversial was 'Pop A Top', a thinly disguised version of a well known soft drink jingle which, like the 'Wincarnis Reggae', sounded just a little too much like a means of obtaining free advertising. Of course ad slogans and product names have become part of pop culture and colloquial expression in Jamaica. It'll be a long time before 'intensified' is permanently buried and 'Dr. No Go' and 'Vigorton' instrumental reggaes have had their run of the Top Twenty. So to get a record played on Jamaican radio and to 'earn' a spot on the hit parade is a growing dilemma for local producers. Even if a hit seems to be on its way up the likelihood of plagiarising is a constant nightmare. Almost days after 'Pop A Top' got going some enterprising bandwagon riders released 'Moma Top' and 'Sister Top'!"

Merry Go Round *The Daily Gleaner* 31st October 1969

From the early Seventies onwards, when people started to come to Jamaica attracted by their love of reggae, they were surprised to find that the Jamaican radio stations did not actually play the type of music that they were expecting to hear. This came as no surprise at all to local record shop proprietors and record producers.

"And you listen to the radio in Jamaica sometimes you wonder if it's a Jamaican station or a New York station." **Winston Edwards**

"It might sound strange but the American influence is so strong in Jamaica that the radio stations won't play these records (deejay records) any more: it's as if the society of Jamaica are ashamed (if not afraid) of the deejay music leaving only the 'rebels' to make it and enjoy it." **Chris Lane**

"When a reggae lover comes to Jamaica he turns the radio on and what does he hear? Surely not the reggae he loves but soul, uptempo versions of reggae standards and an occasional reggae oldies selection. For the hottest hits and the latest releases he has to wait for the weekend top forty or so. The Jamaican radio stations don't push reggae." **Tero Kaski & Pekka Vuorinen**

Writer Tony Rounce, who first visited Kingston in 1974, could not understand why he kept hearing Eric Clapton singing 'I Shot The Sheriff' on Jamaican radio but not the original Bob Marley version.

"Yes, that's quite right about Clapton over Marley. I can also remember being totally aghast that my black step cousins thought it was a good record and even more appalled at the fact that when we went out to the Tit For Tat club it filled the floor every time it was played! It also seemed to be on the radio every time I turned the Rediffusion box on and it was also in the official JBC Top Five which thoroughly disgusted me!

I also remember Jamaican radio generally being mostly quite dull, and really not worth making a concerted effort to listen to unless there was some 'paid programming' on, that's to say a sponsored show, paid for by a producer like Coxsone or whoever... But the new records that I recall hearing on the radio all the time while I was in Kingston (and I was there seven weeks almost) were, apart from 'I Shot The Sheriff', mostly the latest soul 45's: William DeVaughn's 'Be Thankful For What You Got' which was huge. The only Bob Marley record I can recall hearing on the radio was 'Natty Dread' which actually came out while I was there…" **Tony Rounce**

This was possibly due to Alan 'Skill' Cole, Bob Marley's close friend and business associate, attempting to rectify the absence of airplay:

" …and most of what was played on the radio was foreign music. Only Coxsone at Studio One and Duke Reid at Treasure Isle got their records played on the radio so we had to force radio play. Alan 'Skill' Cole was the man who changed that. He said 'We've had enough. It's important for you to play reggae' and he made them an offer they couldn't refuse. Afterwards they played reggae!" **Pete Weston**

"So in that sense we had to use a little muscle, some force to get airplay…"
Alan 'Skill' Cole

"The producer what use them wits will always be the better producer. The one who use him strength can't reach far. Him might have a few tune but you no even hear about them after two weeks… them dead quick. Man what use him wits now him deal with promotion, go down a the radio station, go look 'pon radio play and then check the shop them. The one what use him strength him go bully and bring down all kind of predicament"
Roy 'I Roy' Reid

Perhaps it was because of the cumulative effect of these scandals and forceful tactics that both radio stations discarded their weekly musical charts and neither RJR nor JBC charted sales performance between 1974 and 1978.

A handful of announcers actively supported local talent such as RJR's 'Pipeline' chat show hosted by Neville Willoughby. Other deejays who felt that 'local' music was worth promoting included Jeff 'Free I' Dixon who began working for JBC in 1964 as a radio broadcaster and would play reggae alongside the American and European records. He went on to make a number of records as an artist for Coxsone Dodd at Studio One and Duke Reid at Treasure Isle and radio announcers including Jeff Barnes, Jerry Lewis and Winston Williams also made early 'talkover' records.

"…And some good announcer like Jeff Dixon, who later became 'Free I', used to do a half hour programme in the evening and he went on until he got four hours. He left and then Jeff Barnes take up the slot and Jeff Barnes had another brother who was a cameraman at JBC... Winston Barnes and another brother Ed Barnes who do the sports... Ed Barnes is a freelance now." **Bunny 'Striker' Lee**

Dennis AlCapone recalled the overwhelming influence of Canadian Charlie Babcock who started broadcasting on RJR in May 1959.

"Then this guy from Canada came in called CB, Charlie Babcock, and he's the one who was responsible for most of the jive talks you know. We as deejays later on get our inspiration from CB. He was a white man from Canada. Everybody used to listen to him on RJR and he used to say 'CB the Cool Fool... the guy with the live jive' and he was always jive talking. We used to love to listen to him. (Later) he was in the film 'Smile Orange'. He inspired a lot of other radio deejays..." **Dennis AlCapone**

"Charlie Babcock, a tall, lanky young fellow from Peterborough, Ontario, arrived in Kingston in May 1959 as a disc jockey on the station we then called Radio Jamaica and Rediffusion. He was part of a Canadian invasion instigated by the station's management to fight off the new kid on the block – the Jamaica Broadcasting Corporation... Babcock made the biggest splash of the crew, especially with his 'Platter Parade' late night show 'Night Train'." **Keeble McFarlane**

One of the most important of all Jamaican radio deejays was Michael 'Mikey Dread' Campbell who, paradoxically, did not speak over the airwaves. Mikey first joined JBC in 1976 as a trainee transmitting engineer at a time when the station signed off at midnight and came back on air early the following morning. He approached the management and asked if he could use the time to do an overnight reggae show. Ossie Harvey and Rupert Linton, two senior members of the JBC production department, gave him the go-ahead the following year as long as Mikey did not make any live announcements. The show's time slot was also highly unusual starting at midnight on Sundays and running for four and a half hours. Wholly original and much imitated the 'Dread At The Controls' show broke all the rules by playing the latest 'local' records alongside unreleased dub plates which Mikey would often 'rewind', that is play two or three times in succession, in sound system style.

"I man love versions, love to play twenty piece of on any tune, just to see how ideas can change.... to hear how different man can hear different thing on

the same tune. I man love engineering still, I man love electronics, I man love sound… so it's like I try to develop them things…"
Michael 'Mikey Dread' Campbell

To compensate for the absence of live discourse over four and a half hours he punctuated the music with an extensive, ever expanding, repertoire of sound effects, recorded announcements and jingles made especially for the show by Kingston's top recording stars. Some of these eventually made it on to record, including the 1978 recut of the Treasure Isle standard 'It's Raining' with deejay Ray I, which was released on Carlton Patterson's Black & White label:

"Now if the question being asked is:
'Who is the greatest footballer in the whole wide world?'
There's no other answer to it than the man called Pelé
And if the question being asked is:
'Who is the greatest boxer in the whole wide world?'
There's no other answer to it than the man Muhammad Ali.
And if the question being asked is:
'Who is the greatest operator in the whole wide world?'
There's no other answer to it than the man called Michael Campbell…
Dread at the control tower!"
'Weatherman Skank' Ray I

However, the majority of Mikey's jingles could only be heard on the DATC show despite listeners repeatedly asking Randy's counter staff for the records with "all the effects". While not working at the station Mikey spent a lot of time at the Black Ark, where he recorded singles for Scratch including 'Dread At The Control' and 'Home Guard', and King Tubby's studio where he recorded 'Barber Saloon' and 'Iron Gate Rock' for Carlton Patterson and also obtained and mixed countless 'specials' for his radio show. Cassette tapes of the DATC shows were traded all around the reggae world and Mikey became very popular, not only in Jamaica, but internationally too.

"It was a good programme but the station didn't like it. The people loved it, 'cause it was a first, and they know personally that once them turn on them can plug in them cassette and leave it on till next morning. No chatting, just sound effects and music, music, music. That was the first time they'd had like a roots reggae programme." **Michael 'Mikey Dread' Campbell**

Yet when he was voted Top Radio Personality 1977/78 the out of touch JBC management were visibly shocked and, after increasing tension between Mikey and his supervisors, he resigned from the station in 1979.

"So what I did was write my resignation and, as I give it to them, they just accept it. Yeah... and I man just cool out from the radio right then."
Michael 'Mikey Dread' Campbell

Mikey went on to devote himself full time to his own DATC and Forty Leg record labels and became a highly respected and very successful recording deejay and record producer.

On 1st August 1990 Irie FM 105.5 officially went on air broadcasting from Ocho Rios on Jamaica's North Coast. Some critics said it was impossible to sustain a twenty four hour radio station "that played nothing but reggae music" while others welcomed a station "dedicated to the music that was rejected locally but was accepted by foreigners across borders". Veteran disc jockey Barry 'Barry G' Gordon described Irie FM as "a twenty four version of Dread At The Controls".

"The advent of privately owned radio stations in Jamaica has taken care of the second (that Jamaican radio stations played far more international pop hits than reggae songs. Steve Winwood got airplay in Jamaica; Gregory Isaacs didn't). Reggae musicians always claimed that RJR and JBC radio stifled home grown recording artists by tilting their playlists toward American and British pop stars. When the government opened radio frequencies for private ownership during the Eighties that picture began to change. Irie FM, broadcasting from Ocho Rios, is the reggae island's first all reggae radio station, providing airplay for Jamaican artists day and night."
Brian Jahn & Tom Weber

Irie FM finally gave reggae music complete coverage in the land of its birth... "you have a lot of stations now"... and there are now over twenty radio stations with round the clock broadcasting. Irie FM has proved to be a massive success for "never before has Jamaica and her people been exposed to Jamaican culture and music in the way Irie FM has done it." As always, it has proved completely impossible to please all of the people all of the time and producers like Bunny Lee now yearn for the 'good old days' when he was able to 'phone in requests from the front desks of RJR and JBC.

"Even now in Jamaica the underworld guys that have the money can pay an announcer a million dollars to play one tune because they're washing their money. So it's Number One whether it sold or not and the sound man say 'What is the Number One tune?' And they start to play it…

But the deejays nowadays plug themselves…most of the deejays in Jamaica you don't hear them say the singers' names. Very few announcers do that! Just call themselves the dance hall master. You understand? So it's just hype. You just hear about those people (the deejays) and you don't hear about who writes or sings the song and that. The old time announcers would say 'That was sung by Slim Smith… and The Aggrovators' and then they'd call all The Aggrovators' names. And people hear about them and want to know who The Aggrovators are …when you introduce the music and the people at least (that way) they'd know them…" **Bunny 'Striker' Lee**

Until the inception of Irie FM the Jamaican radio stations had maintained a love hate relationship with local music. Some would say that they loved to hate it and both RJR and JBC were usually regarded as little more than tools of the establishment. The record producers had to either fight or pay, whether legally or illegally, to have their records played on the radio and the sound systems and juke boxes did far more to promote 'local' music. However, it can be argued, that both stations' insistence on playing almost anything but Jamaican music actually proved to be a major contributing factor to the all encompassing, always inclusive, nature of the music that was created on the island during the Fifties, Sixties and Seventies.

"It should be remembered that Jamaican radio followed a policy of playing USA style radio friendly pop, country & western and uptown soul almost to the exclusion of 'local' tunes and, although this brainwashing influence from the stations informed Jamaica's musical tastes, it arguably helped to create Jamaican music in most of the forms that we know it." **Chris Lane**

The arguments can never be resolved but the power of radio broadcasting cannot be denied. Whether the radio stations regularly played 'local' music or not it was in the studios of RJR and JBC that the earliest stirrings of ska, a completely new and totally original genre of music, were first recorded.

RJR (Radio Jamaica Rediffusion)
32 Lyndhurst Road
Kingston 5

Engineers include:
Lynford 'Andy Capp' Anderson, Graeme Goodall,
Keith 'Sticky' Parks & Hol Plummer

JBC (Jamaica Broadcasting Corporation)
5 South Odeon Avenue
Half Way Tree
Kingston 10

Engineers include:
Louis Burke, Desmond Elliott, Graeme Goodall,
Ossie Harvey & Graham Watt

Chapter 4

Noel Hawks

Chapter 4
Federal Country... Another Hit!
Records Ltd & Federal Records

"Federal was the key to the whole record industry. Everything revolved round there." **Byron Lee**

"We were screaming but we weren't smart enough to keep a record of all this. It wasn't something we saw as historical. We didn't think we were creating history... we were caught up in the moment. That's the sad part of Federal!" **Paul Khouri**

Ken Khouri, born in 1917, the youngest child in his family with three older sisters, grew up in Kingston. His mother was born in Jamaica of Cuban parents and his father was born in Lebanon and came to Jamaica at the age of twelve. Mr Khouri senior owned drapery and haberdashery stores in rural Jamaica and a furniture store in Kingston. After leaving school Ken began work for a friend of the family, Mr Joseph Issa, who owned drapers shops and, more importantly, juke boxes which were situated all over the island. Vincent Chin of Randy's Records also began his career working with Mr Issa's jukebox operation. Ken Khouri then opened his own furniture store on West Street, Kingston and, although he was always musically inclined, he actually became involved in the business "by accident". In 1949 he had taken his father to Miami "for his illness" and was in a radio shop when a "distressed man" came in trying to sell a Presto portable disc recorder to raise the money to fly back to California. Apparently the radio shop proprietor was not interested but Ken Khouri was and he purchased the recorder, amplifier and recording blanks from the man for $350. On returning to Jamaica he began to use the system in his home to record people's messages to send to friends and relations who had emigrated and he would also travel to weddings, including that of Ivan Chin and Lily Chuck, to record the ceremony for thirty shillings (£1.50).

"I will try to retell the information my father Ken Khouri gave me. It started off with him acquiring a cutting machine. It was like a small dub machine; a very primitive one compared to the one we have today. He bought it in Florida and brought it back to Jamaica in 1949. It was the first cutting machine imported to the island and he travelled around the whole country with the machine. What he did first was to record greetings on a lacquer disc, which is known as a dub plate today, so that they can send it to families and friends who had emigrated to other countries like England. He did it for thirty shillings." **Paul Khouri**

However, the demand for making musical recordings soon became overwhelming, and Ken Khouri stated "I became like a music machine Pied Piper… people used to follow me home and I would record until two or three am". Graeme Goodall takes up the story.

"But during this time I met Ken Khouri. Ken had gone up to Miami to buy a car, evidently, and he was wandering around and I think next to the car dealership he wandered into a pawnshop. A guy, a musician, had just come in and pawned a Presto portable disc recorder, with a supply of like twenty blank discs and so Ken asked me 'What's this?' and I explained it to him. I think he had like a half an hour with this musician who had pawned this thing and he packed it all up in the back of this Ford Fairlane, which he'd bought, and brought it back to Jamaica; the idea being that he was going to record people and teach Stanley Motta a thing or two. But of course he'd forgotten, or at least nobody bothered to tell him, that in the meantime disc recording had been bypassed and there was tape recording." **Graeme Goodall**

After moving into a club at Red Gal Ring in the parish of St Andrew, which had the space required to record a band, Ken began to record local mento artists for his Kalypso (no connection with the UK Melodisc subsidiary of the same name) and Capitol labels. "I bought down equipment from California... just one microphone. One track."

"In the beginning it was monaural only and everything had to be done in one take. There was no over dubbing of horns etc. When we had our 78's done in England we used to record in his back porch. We worked very late at night because there was too much noise from the streets in the daytime, you know, like cars, birds, and so on. There were guitar, banjo, rhumba box which played the bass part, bamboo sax which was created and played by Sugar Belly. My dad recorded the music straight to a lacquer disc so if any noise from the streets was recorded by mistake they had to start all over again... also if there was one mistake in the studio we had to start all over again." **Paul Khouri**

Initially Ken Khouri established a connection with Decca Records in London to manufacture 78rpm records from his acetates and his first 'local' release was 'Naughty Little Flea' by Lord Flea on the Capitol label.

"... the first attempt was a real gamble. But when I got to King Street the Saturday I saw a line two blocks long. We sold out in less than two weeks." **Ken Khouri**

"Then he got this great idea to record music. He found tough mento bands, got the music done on lacquer discs, sent them to Decca Records in England and got 78's manufactured there and sent back to him. He said that the first song he did was Lord Flea's 'Naughty Little Flea'. He sold records in a place called Times Store with a gentleman called Alec Durie. That was one of the most popular retail stores on King Street in downtown Kingston. They were selling drinks, toys, all kinds of things in those days. And those records were on the label called Times." **Paul Khouri**

The records sold "for between four and five shillings" (20p and 25p) and the success of these first mento recordings encouraged Ken to begin manufacturing his own records. He contacted a Californian company who sold him two record presses and also sent an expert to Kingston along with the machinery to teach Ken the intricacies of the recording and

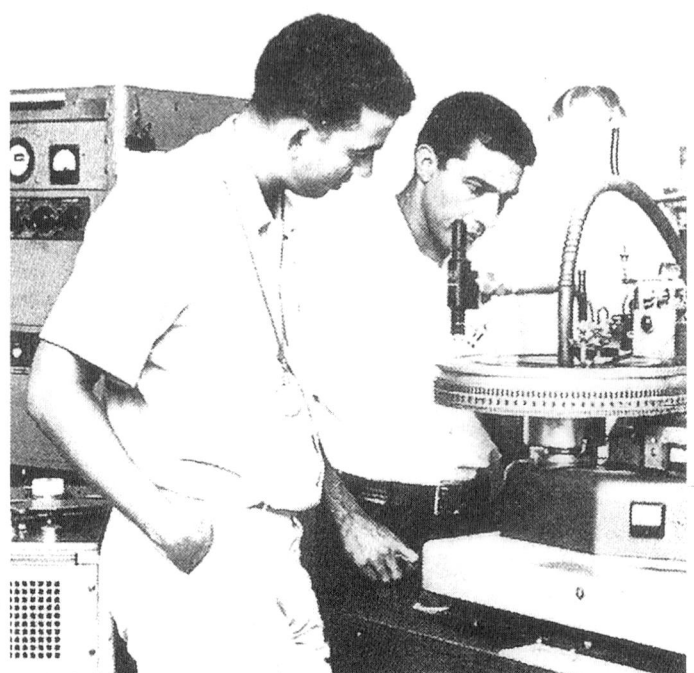
Louis 'Buddy' Davidson and Richard Khouri at Federal Recording Studio

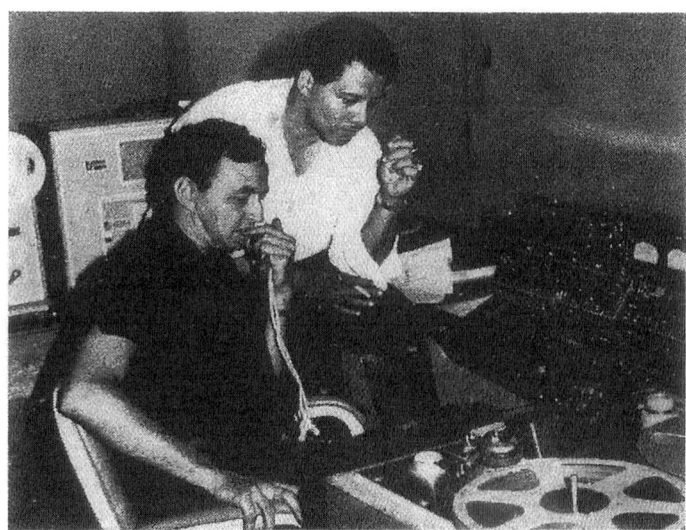
Graeme Goodall and Byron Lee at Federal Recording Studio

manufacturing processes. After phasing out his furniture store in 1954 he started Records Ltd and began to manufacture "the first locally pressed records on the island".

"One day Ken Khouri went to Alec Durie and said 'Why not try manufacturing our own records by ourselves in Jamaica? Will you invest some money?' Alec Durie had great faith in my dad so he agreed on it. My father went to California to do research on record pressing plants and machinery so that he could create one in Jamaica. It was how Jamaica's first pressing plant was created. The factory was called Records Ltd built on 129 King Street near Times Store. It was around 1954. Now he did not need to wait three months just to get five hundred records from England. He could make them in a day. And then he started his own Kalypso label. By November of the same year he had the first locally pressed records available in Jamaica. And not only that he then acquired major US labels like Mercury. You know, got the licence to manufacture and sell American music in Jamaica. So his business came to involve more than local music like those early mento recordings." **Paul Khouri**

Two contemporary accounts from *The Daily Gleaner* recount the full details:

"Jamaica's calypso singers are advertising the island's music, mirth and manner of life in many countries of the world: for to all the lands from which come vacationists they take on their departure from Jamaica the lusty tunes and witty words of native calypsonians.

While calypso records as souvenirs help to 'sell' the idea of Jamaica as a holiday land the local production of calypso records, as well as the stamping of records of popular tunes from the United States, is fostering a community of industries.

There is recording, album manufacture and label printing all three of which go into the production of discs made and distributed in Jamaica by Records Ltd. This three month old music firm's experience is that its making available in the island local calypso records has not lifted this type of music to top place among resident record collectors. They still prefer popular United States tunes...

Mr Ken Khouri, managing director of Records Ltd, told the Gleaner that production targets had not yet been achieved but he is satisfied that the locally stamped record is filling two needs. He said: 'It is enabling the local singer to reach a wider public here in the island as well as outside of Jamaica; also it is bringing to the Jamaican public the latest 'hits' from the United States far more rapidly than when we relied entirely on importers to bring in the records. Within a day or two of the master stamper arriving here discs from it are available to record shops. This means that inside of a week of a record being released in the States it can be bought in Jamaica.'

Mr Khouri went on to say that in the sale of records time is a great factor. Usually buyers want tunes they hear at the motion pictures and over the radio. They request them as soon as they hear them. When there is a time lag of three to four months, as is the case of importing records, the buyer's tastes pass on to newer tunes.

Local record production by Mr Khouri, who is a pioneer in this field has vastly increased since Records Ltd commenced operations. The company which has pioneer status holds exclusive right to stamp records issued by Mercury Recordings Corporation of Chicago. According to Records Ltd's experience the most popular United States musicians with the Jamaican public this year are Patti Page, Ralph Marterie, The Crew Cuts, Georgia Gibbs and The David Carroll Orchestra."

The Daily Gleaner 19th June 1954

"Records Ltd soon to open at 129 King Street in September 1954. Gramophone record production is soon to be commenced in Jamaica by Records Ltd. This is a new enterprise headed by Mr Alec Durie, Managing Director of the Jamaica Times Ltd, Messrs Anthony Hart of Montego Bay and Mr. Ken Khouri who has been appointed manager of Records Ltd. Records Ltd have obtained a licence to stamp the full catalogue of Mercury Records. A chromium plated copper disc is the mould or stamper. Into it is placed the record 'biscuit'. A second copper mould is placed above and pressure applied. Both sides of the record are stamped in a single operation...

Records Ltd also planned to make recordings of local compositions. In that case tape recordings would be sent to the processors overseas. From

these stampers would be made and returned here for records to be pressed for commercial gain. Records Ltd Jamaica made records that would not be cheaper than the imported discs the Gleaner was also told. The advantage of processing locally was not a matter of economy in money but of making records available more quickly to buyers here."
The Daily Gleaner 17th September 1954

"I was in advertising in an office at 129 King Street and Ken Khouri was in an alcove below me. He said 'come and listen to my first record'. 'Skokiaan' (by August Msarurgwa/Musarurwa) was the first record they made. Before that we used to import records and there were only three stores that sold them: DePass Enterprises, Times Store and Stanley Motta. Ken would get hit records from overseas and produce them in Jamaica and Byron Lee later did the same thing." **Ronnie Nasralla**

The following year Ken purchased a Magnecord one track tape recorder and three channel mixer and, with the assistance of Graeme Goodall, set up a recording studio with separate recording and control rooms in an outbuilding at Upper King Street. With both the Caribbean Recording Company Ltd and Ken Khouri's Records Limited operating in Kingston the cost of manufacturing records dropped considerably. Making records became far easier and Ken Khouri's Federal Records brought together many of the previously disparate elements into one unified whole.

"So Ken and I were talking and we became firm friends. Poppa Khouri as we called him... Poppa Koo. And so he went back up and bought a Magnecorder recorder and I think like a box of tapes, and he said 'Well when can we do this?' By this time he was pressing 78rpm records from stampers for Mercury Records that were sent down from America so he's the first person who started pressing records in Jamaica. Anyway we went out the back of his record pressing plant, which was in Upper King Street, and we found an old outbuilding. It was like a ramshackle old sort of outhouse thing, with termites running up and down the wall and everything, but I got the bright idea that I'd strengthen the walls by pouring sand down them to give me some sort of isolation. I remember we poured sand in there and it went well until I got about six feet up the wall and the whole wall collapsed so I thought I'd better go back and re-examine the engineering of this thing. So we filled it up with fibreglass and anything else we could find and we had this Magnecorder with a three channel mixer and Ken went on recording… he recorded calypsos and things like this. But it was an attempt, you know, it was a start." **Graeme Goodall**

In 1957 the operation relocated to 220 Foreshore Road, later renamed Marcus Garvey Drive, on an industrial estate in the Hagley Park district of Kingston and Records Ltd became a subsidiary of the Federal Record Manufacturing Co Ltd. An article in The Gleaner stated that the directors were Alec Durie, Anthony Hart and Kenneth Khouri (Managing Director) and Mrs Gloria Khouri was appointed Secretary of the Company who employed "about twenty workers in the office and the factory... Almost every kind of record including 78 and 45 rpm 45 Extended Play and $33^{1/3}$ RPM records of ten and twelve inches will be manufactured by the Company..." The new company made records for Records Limited, distributors of Mercury and Kalypso/Calypso Records; Kentone Limited, distributors for American Decca and British Brunswick; GloKen Company Limited, distributors of Capitol Records; Phonodisc Limited, distributors for Herald and Ember Records as well as Monogram Rhythm & Blues Records.

"Ken moved the recording equipment from the studio on King Street to Foreshore Road which is called Marcus Garvey Drive now. He set up Federal Record Manufacturing there and then the recording studio in 1958. It was the first real studio in Jamaica. It was a small wooden building with a zinc roof. The studio had Ampex recording machines and an Altec broadcasting console because he could not afford to buy really sophisticated recording equipment. But he had a lot of good microphones like Neumann, Beyer and Sennheiser. They were not very expensive. He also had an RCA condenser microphone to record low frequency instruments like bass or trombone." **Paul Khouri**

The studio, right beside the pressing plant, was a "very primitive, small wooden building with a zinc roof. Recordings were mainly done at night to avoid the daily noise of the traffic".

"It was all a process of learning; he did his best. He got information from many people who could help him. He associated with qualified technicians like the Australian Graeme Goodall who was educated in England in the field of electrical engineering. He could build and fix amplifiers and stuff. He had great knowledge of the efficiencies of electronic equipment so he could teach my dad how to get the most out of whatever he was using without creating distortion."   **Paul Khouri**

"When I decided to leave Radio Jamaica I went to see Ken because he really wanted to get into it and he'd already started building Federal Records down in Tinson Pen. So he said 'Well let's build a studio' and I went in there and he had an Ampex I believe, a 351, and a four channel mixer and we sort of worked out of two rooms. We had air conditioners, wall units that we used to switch off during recording, and we'd record it for two minutes and forty five seconds. Then we'd switch the recorder off and then switch the air conditioning back on… and again the four channel mixer. So I said 'Ken we've got to do something about this. We need echo'. So he said 'Well what are you going to do?' so I said 'Well I'll modify this mixer…' We went down to Times Store in King Street, Lower King Street, which was owned by Alec Durie, who was one of the original investors in Federal Records, and we begged an old RCA amplifier from him and a speaker. And we put that up and a microphone which I believe I stole from Radio Jamaica (please don't tell anybody!) and we put this in and I tried to get some Jamaican masons to actually build a room without any parallel surfaces.

I had a lot of problems with brick masons in Jamaica, telling them to get their walls unparallel. They build great houses… telling them to build the walls at different angles… it just didn't make sense to them. They could not understand this crazy white guy who spoke funny telling them to build a room like they'd never built before where nothing was parallel… everything was angled. Anyway, it worked quite well…

I had one occasion where I had noise in the mixer and I couldn't figure out what it was. It was at night time and I was recording somebody… I think it was Byron Lee. And there was this terrible chirping noise and eventually, it took me about an hour to track it down, I found there was a cricket that had got up inside the speaker and he was singing along with the music! And of course when I went in to check it he said 'Oh-oh, human being coming through this little door I've got to keep quiet now' and he'd keep quiet. And he'd keep quiet till we started recording again then he'd start chirping again!"   **Graeme Goodall**

At first the majority of the recordings made at the Federal studio were never intended for commercial release but were meant strictly for sound system play on acetate, reference disc or what would later be termed 'dub plates'.

"He gave Coxsone Wednesdays and Duke Reid Thursdays for their recordings. On Fridays he made dub plates for producers and sound system owners. Mondays and Tuesdays he made accessible to the poor and working class producers who could only afford to book by the hour."
Prince Buster

Graeme Goodall, now Federal's chief recording engineer, set aside Fridays at Federal Studios solely for cutting acetates. The sound system operators would occasionally sell these to other sound systems but only to those operators who were not perceived to be serious competition.

"… the sound system boys would also sell their dubs to their 'friendly' sound systems. Like Prince Buster would never sell to anybody in Kingston but he would sell it to somebody in Spanish Town or somebody in Port Royal or somebody in Old Harbour. Likewise Duke Reid, likewise Coxsone and Smith and all these people they would sell it to, you know, their non-competitive, shall we say, sound system.

And I used to have to cut these dubs, as they called them, or direct references on this old mono lathe and Friday was the dub day. 'Cause sound systems always work Friday night, Saturday night and Sunday and I didn't record anything on a Friday because I needed the equipment to cut records. The acetates… Papa Khouri, as we used to call him, he used to sell these to the guys, you know, and I remember it was thirty shillings each… one pound ten shillings (£1.50) each.

So, anyway, we had that and we had one tape recorder. We had a Neumann disc cutting lathe and we'd record Monday through Thursday and then Friday was 'dub' day. And these record producers, who in those days were sound system men like Coxsone, Duke Reid, Smith Hi-Lite, who of course also had liquor concessions so they used to run the sound systems basically as a non-profit thing. It was the old 'loss leader' thing, you know, and they instigated it. They did a loss leader so they could sell the liquor at these dances and, of course, to get the people to the dances

DISC-MAKING PLANT HERE

INCREASED productivity in the island's rapidly expanding industrialisation pattern was marked this week by the opening of the Federal Record Manufacturing Co. Ltd., another important factory for record pressing which provides clear evidence of the phenomenal growth of the Industrial Development Corporation's Industrial Estate, says an I.D.C. release.

Directors of the new record manufacturing factory are Messrs Alec Durie, Anthony Hart and Kenneth Khouri (Mr. Khouri being the Managing Director) Mrs Gloria Khouri has been appointed Secretary of the Company.

'Situated at 220 Foreshore Road — in an easily accessible section of the Industrial Estate — the factory is a well-equipped up to date building covering 5,000 sq ft and plans for further construction expansion have been provided.

Almost every kind of record — including 78 and 45 RPM, 45 Extended Play, and 33 1/3 RPM records of 10 and 12 inches — will be manufactured by the Company who have been granted the franchise. (Continued on PAGE 17)

Disc-making plant here

From Page One

chise for distribution throughout the West Indies.

"The parent company will manufacture records for various distributing companies which have been formed. These include Records Limited distributors of Mercury and Calypso records, Kentone Limited distributors for Decca of the US and Brunswick of Britain; GloKen Company Limited, distributors of Capitol Records; Phonodisc Limited, distributors for Herald and Ember Records; as well as Monogram Rhythm and Blues records.

"The Federal Record Manufacturing Co. are now fully equipped to record for individual interests, employing a staff of about twenty workers in the office and factory. They anticipate reaching peak production in just over a month from the opening date.

"With a modern, acoustically-perfect studio where weekly disc jockey shows will be a main feature of the Company's newest record-manufacturing techniques, Mr. Ken Khouri disclosed this week that the Company is to a large extent a reality due to the hard work, excellent cooperation and technical assistance accorded by IDC officials, with whom he has worked in close collaboration to effect completion of the factory."

they had to have a killer sound system so that's how that all started. Then of course Prince Buster came in and he didn't have a liquor concession but he'd work with other liquor suppliers and he was probably one of the funniest and nicest guys I've ever met in my life… I talked to him on the telephone probably a year or so ago. I have very fond memories of Prince Buster. Poppa Khouri and he could not get on, you know, and actually Poppa Khouri threw him out of Federal Records but something rang a bell, you know, a case when you meet somebody and a bell rings and you say 'there's something more here'. And I went and pleaded with Poppa Koo… I said 'Please let me handle it' and he said 'No, no, no he's a trouble maker. He's always causing grief'. I said 'Let me work with him, let me work with him', you know, 'I'll be responsible' and from then on even though Prince Buster and I fought, I mean there's no two ways about it Prince Buster fought with everybody, but since then there's been a deep friendship and tremendous respect, I hope, both ways." **Graeme Goodall**

"Prince Buster used to record there too. Most of Prince Buster's big tunes were done at Federal." **Bunny 'Striker' Lee**

Federal Records was not only the place for the sound system men to record but it was also where they had their records pressed too. Many of these early Jamaican seven inch 45rpm releases, including those on the Coxsone, Prince Buster, Duke Reid's and Treasure Isle labels, were overprinted 'Manufactured By Federal Record Mfg Co Ltd Jamaica WI'.

"Federal… everyone used to record there then. Coxsone and Duke Reid put out their own things but Federal never distributed those things… That was how Mr Khouri start with a little place. You understand? And that became his empire… started from scratch and it gradually grew." **Bunny 'Striker' Lee**

"In the early days everybody had to use Federal Studio because there were not any other studios around. So everybody like Coxsone, Duke Reid, Prince Buster, Sonia Pottinger, King Edwards used Federal Studio. My dad rented it out to people who could afford to pay the price. And he also set a special low price for those who could not afford the price like Prince Buster. At one time Federal had two studios: the original one at Marcus Garvey Drive and the other on Bell Road." **Paul Khouri**

Federal had an almost total monopoly on record pressing in Jamaica but, initially, they had to send to New York or Miami for mastering and, apparently, the masters for Coxsone's first ever session with Roland Alphonso were lost in transit and never found.

"Federal used to cut in Jamaica but at first if a man wanted a stamper you used to have to go to 'foreign' to get it cut. You'd send to Miami and they'd make the stamper."   **Bunny 'Striker' Lee**

Graeme Goodall recalled that the recordings had to come in at just under three minutes, not only because of the strictures of needing to immediately grasp the dancers' attention and continue holding it, but also for a more pragmatic reason: "That was all that I could squeeze onto the disc at one hundred and ten lines per inch and still get the bottom end they wanted".

"You notice that everything was two minutes and fifty seconds? You ever noticed that? There's a very good reason. To get the bass on the disc I had to cut it at one hundred and ten lines per inch on this old Neumann fixed pitch lathe. And to get a decent level on it I'd have to cut it at that pitch and that pitch ran out at two minutes and fifty seconds."   **Graeme Goodall**

In 1963 Ken Khouri expanded the Federal studio. Graeme Goodall supervised the building in brick with a proper echo chamber , brought the first stereo equipment to Jamaica, and began making stereo records. Federal could now master mono records but their stereo recordings still had to be mastered in the USA. Years later he recalled:

"When it comes to the history of Federal Records you have to divide it into stages. The small studio was the centre for the ska era. I took a primitive Ampex tube four channel mixer and upgraded it with another three channels with an echo feed on each. This gave me three channels straight... three channels with echo and one channel for echo return. The bass, played by Lloyd Brevett, was a 'stand-up' and I used a RCA 44 bx ribbon on it. But any fool can put stuff on tape. The trick was to put it down onto acetate and make it sound the way the public wanted to hear it at the sound system dances. That's why I went out to these dances so that I could 'capture' the sound the way they wanted to hear it. The disc cutter was a fixed pitch Neumann lathe with a Grampian MQY mono cutter driven by a Gotham amp. I happened to meet George Piros, the master cutter at Fine Recording

Studios in NYC. He advised me to warm up the cutting head by feeding straight tone into it for about five minutes... 'Get them coils and armature loosened up, man'... and purge the damping fluid that Grampian supplied, replace it with high quality brake fluid, administered with a special hypodermic needle cut to size so that the fluid would actually get down to the armature instead of bopping around the magnets."
Graeme Goodall

"Then the two track era came; we did one shot recording. We overdubbed voice… whatever we needed. We recorded on two track to two track… bouncing two track to two track. Constant overdubbing increased the noise of the tape and the signal to noise ratio had to be very good to avoid ending up more noise than music! It was not like today when we make music piece by piece." **Paul Khouri**

"Anyway, meanwhile, I talked Ken into getting an Ampex 352, which is a stereo recorder. Would you believe this was the second recorder he got? You know, oh wow, two recorders! And then I wired up another mixer so we could actually record in stereo in this same little Federal Records studio. Then I had Byron Lee in to put down the brass line in the kitchen so we could get some natural reverb on it and we recorded it at night. And of course the first stereo record was 'Joy Ride In Stereo' but Ken Khouri wasn't too certain about stereo so we did a mono version called 'Joy Ride In Hi-Fi'. There was one jacket printed and the stereo ones had 'stereo' stickers stuck over the 'Hi-Fi'. The jacket was designed by Ronnie Nasralla and when it came out... the first stereo record of Byron Lee... believe me... it caused a tremendous sensation with the people who at that time were just promoting from their hi-fi record players to stereo. And all of a sudden here's a local one, you know, and I did all the stupid ping pongy effects, you know. I mean it was very primitive but in those days you tended to do that to demonstrate that you were recording stereo...that was the trick.

And we used to do another trick: we used to take two reverb feeds and feed in whatever instruments we had on the left then we'd bring the reverb back on the right hand channel and vice versa. George Piros of Fine Recording in New York taught me that little trick. In the meantime I'd met a very incredible man, who I still count as a very great friend, Tommy Dowd. Byron Lee introduced him to me because Byron was handling Atlantic Records in Jamaica. So Tom Dowd became my mentor more than anybody in the

world as far as innovative, imaginary or imaginative, techniques in recording and I respect Tommy for that because he was an innovator. People don't realise, other than Les Paul, Tom Dowd was the first person to make an eight track tape recorder out of old Ampex 350 machines."
Graeme Goodall

Federal were justifiably proud of their stereo recording equipment and supplied in depth details under the heading 'Technical Information' on a number of their long playing releases from the period.

"Recorded by Federal Record Studios, Kingston 11, Jamaica. Recording Engineer: Graeme Goodall. For best results playback equipment should be adjusted to, or near RIAA characteristics. This recording was made on Ampex 354 multi-channel tape recorder. Microphones used included Neumann U67 condenser and U47 condenser."
'Authentic Jamaican Folk Songs'

"All recordings were made in the Number Two Studio of Federal Records, Kingston, Jamaica using Neumann Condensor, RCA ribbons, Beyer and EV dynamics microphones, a custom built Altec 16 channel mixer and Ampex 351/2 tape recorders." **'Space Flight'**

"For best results playback equipment should be adjusted to, or near to, RIAA characteristics. Microphones used included Neumann V47 & V67 condensors, RCA 44BX and 77DX ribbons, EV666 and Beyer M66 dynamics feeding direct to a Custom built 10 Channel Altec Mixer. The sessions were recorded on Ampex 354 multi channel and 350 single channel recorded at 15 inches per second. The organ used was a Lowry S552 Lincolnwood Deluxe Model with a Leslie cabinet attachment. Produced by: Kenneth Khouri, Recording Engineer: Byron Smith, Musical Director: Byron Lee, Recorded at: Federal Studios, Pressed by Federal Record Manufacturing Company Limited, 220 Marcus Garvey Drive, Kingston 11, Dominion Of Jamaica." **'Jamaica Ska'**

And the Federal seven inch covers from the time proudly boast "Another Hit! The Fully Air Conditioned Recording & Television Studio… Federal Record Manufacturing Company Ltd."

Chapter 4

A second studio was constructed with sufficient room to accommodate an orchestra for local film, advertising and recording companies. Federal continued to expand and consolidate its pole position until Coxsone opened Studio One, with a one track board purchased from Federal when they upgraded to two track, and George Benson, Bunny Rae and Edward Seaga's WIRL (West Indies Records Limited) both began to challenge Federal's almost complete control of Kingston's recording and record manufacturing industry.

"Yes. Coxsone bought a lot of stuff from my dad because my dad was advanced. He sold it to him very inexpensively. Coxsone and my dad were very close. As a matter of fact, without meaning anything, my dad said to him 'You are my first black son.' My father loved him a lot, and he treated my dad very well too, so both of them got on well although we were competitive in a friendly and loving way. My dad sold him whatever he wanted… sometimes gave him. My dad had a very soft spot for Coxsone. We called him an old timer! We had a close rapport continuously with each other."
Paul Khouri

"So I met Bunny Rae and George Benson, who had started WIRL, West Indies Records Limited, with Eddie Seaga and on a couple of trips back to Jamaica (luckily enough my wife worked for an airline so it wasn't too expensive) I helped them out with their studio. It was a little smaller than the original Federal one. In the meantime Ken Khouri had built the big studio at Federal and then Byron Smith came on board. I worked with him at Radio Jamaica, he was one of my protégés there and he'd had enough time with them so Ken Khouri said 'Well who can you get to operate the small studio while you work the big one?' The big one was a three track studio, believe it or not: Scully three track… and I modified an Altec console with two separate Altec mini mixers. For echo I used Altec 604B monitors."
Graeme Goodall

"Federal was the place until WIRL set up a little studio… and the work started to share. When WIRL was going on Federal were going on too, you know, because the record business started to get so big so some went to Dynamics… it was WIRL before Dynamics run by a man named Bunny Rae and George Benson who later opened Record Specialists with his wife. You understand? So the work could share and people like we would go to any studio you could get but, at the time, Federal and WIRL used to be the manufacturers. They cut stampers…" **Bunny 'Striker' Lee**

"When they built the big studio, everything was going great. And then West Indies Records Limited (WIRL) was owned by Eddie Seaga and he attempted to get into this and, strangely enough, because Smithy (Byron Smith) and I virtually had the market sewn up there was only one place to record….

By that time for the small studio Ken had I bought a Neumann U47 microphone, which he made me take out every night and hand to him personally. Then he'd take it home with him and guard it with this firearm under the pillow and he'd bring it back the next day to me. Have you ever heard the story about Mr Goodie's iron pipe?

Well, a few of these boys got into a fight in the studio one day and they started swinging things around and someone had a Red Stripe bottle and he broke it and he was going after Prince Buster I think. And the two of them were at it and all the musicians around, typical Jamaica thing, they love a fight and they'll egg each side on but they're not going to get involved too much. So there they were circling and I thought 'Oh my God!' I ran into the studio and this fight looked as if it was going to get a little bit frantic so I stood up to the Neumann to protect it, that's what I was doing, my mind was on the microphone. And I said 'Wait a minute I'm unarmed' so I ran out to the factory and the only thing I could find was a piece of three quarter inch electrical conduit about three feet long. So I grabbed that and ran back to the studio and said 'First blood clot man come to this place get a lick with the pipe'. I was now standing flashing around with this three foot piece of pipe and all of a sudden everybody stopped and looked at me and broke into hysterics. They all cracked up… fell apart on the floor. This skinny little guy, I weighed one hundred and forty seven pounds at the time… ten stone seven… and so there's Goody standing up with the iron pipe protecting his Neumann.

The next day I came in and you wouldn't believe it. They'd gone out and got a bicycle handle grip and they'd put it on the pipe; they'd painted it all up and put tape all around it and ribbons and presented it to me and, from that time, Mr Goodie was never there unless the iron pipe was there… so some of the musicians will remember Mr Goodie's iron pipe!

So, anyway, Ken made the big studio. Perry Henzell was producing films and film commercials at the time and Ken did a deal with Perry to shoot all his commercials... video commercials. JBC had started television at that time. Donald Wellington, who I knew very well, another apprentice of mine, took over as Director of Engineering for JBC Television. And so this is why the studio was as large as it was. Probably, in hindsight, a little bit too big for what we wanted or what we needed but, however, it worked. It had a classic sound but, strangely enough, the local people preferred the old studio sound. Yeah, I think it was the closeness of the musicians... while the musicians in the big studio tended to be more spaced out, spaced out in their mind as well as in their bodies, but, you know, there's too much distance between them and they liked the small studio which Byron Smith, 'Smithy', was running. And it's rather interesting that Byron Smith had a signature, as did I, and you can tell distinctly the sound that you got. You know, the sound that I got was different to Smithy's and no matter who we were producing for we still had that signature, although it may have been modified on the top, but deep down inside you could tell if you listen."

Graeme Goodall

"As an aside....until the mid Sixties Jamaica's power was 110 volts, 40 hz. This meant that we had to use rotary convertors for all speed dependent devices...particularly US manufactured Ampex recorders. Then the marvellous government experts decided to convert the whole island to 110 volt 50 hz. Isn't that typical! So it was into the machine shop to make sleeves for all the capstan motors and install auto transformers so that the electronics would perform to spec. Remember, we were still essentially in the tube era."   **Graeme Goodall**

Perhaps Graeme had forgotten that Stanley Motta was one of those "marvellous government experts"...

"My father was known as 'Fifty Cycle Motta' as he was a driving force in getting the cycle changed from the forty cycle current and, because of the proximity of the USA, the government went to the US cycle."

Brian Motta

"Federal Records, Poppa Koo, Ken Khouri, was convinced to build a 'big' combo audio/video studio by Perry Henzell who had started Vista Films (Perry directed 'The Harder They Come' with Jimmy Cliff) basically to produce TV commercials for JBC TV that had just gone on air. It had a full lighting grid and perfectly flat floor for tracking. However, the commercial market didn't develop as well as expected and the audio recording side took over.

I equipped it with a ten channel Altec 'green monster', still tube, backed with two smaller Altec mono mixers as echo send/returns. For echo I used a Fairchild spring unit with an interesting modification developed by Pepe Rush of Rush Electronics in the UK. We inserted a light dependent resistor between the output from the springs and the input to the output amplifier. Sounds convoluted but it's the only way that I can describe it. The LDR was activated by a combo incandescent bulb and a neon tube fired by the input amp. In this way we could vary the attack time and the unit was virtually quiet when no signal was present. We also had tie lines to the original live chamber.

But I digress. I was extremely careful with the acoustics. It was basically a 3x4x5 dimension room but I used elliptical diffusers and strategically placed bass absorption units developed by EMI. I designed gobo incorporating the same bass absorbers and faced on the reverse side with acoustic aluminium from Alcan....so I had a reflective/absorptive depending on which side the instrument was facing. About this time electronic guitar and bass amps were coming into use (Ampeg bass and Fender guitar) so I went further into the use of DI which I had used from the old RJR recording days. I found that Ampex used a wonderful input transformer in their 350 series recorders. (I think they may have been designed by Dean Jensen but I'm not sure). This gave me a Hi impedance/Lo impedance matching unit. But the secret was to use the DI in combination with a microphone feed. In this way I could get the attack/sustain sound that I wanted. The control room monitors were Altec 604D driven by HH Scott tube amps. I found that they were so mid-range deficient that when you actually put it down on disc they were so hot that they jumped out at you.

At the same time the small studio was being handled by Byron 'Smitty' Smith an engineer I had trained at RJR. I have to admit that when it came to laying down ska/rock steady tracks he beat me hands down. Isn't that the way it should be....the student excels the teacher? He was responsible for all the great Treasure Isle material. He eventually went on to work for Duke Reid at Treasure Isle Studios down on Bond Street." **Graeme Goodall**

Byron 'Baron'/'Smithy' Smith had been taught by Graeme Goodall but Ken Khouri kept things in the family too and two of his sons Richard, who was born 1943, and Paul who was born in 1946, also joined Federal Records.

"I was born in Jamaica in 1946 so I'm 63 years old (2009). I actually studied plastics extrusion (a high volume manufacturing process in which raw plastic is melted and formed into a continuous profile) for PVC tubing. Dad thought it was the way to go and we're pioneers in that too! But it was always music... I studied music for six or seven years and played keyboards, drums and percussion. It was in the blood. I got bored with the plastics business and got into the music, convinced my dad, and I started producing records.

I was the technical son so I was trained by a German named Eckhardt Krieger. He came to Jamaica, fell in love with the place, and taught me so I'm also a mastering engineer. He also taught me how to use and maintain the equipment. This would have been in 1961/62 as rhythm & blues was turning into ska and I was involved in the early Byron Lee sessions with Monty Morris and The Maytals at the Federal Studios. There was nowhere else to go at the time! I was very young and very eager and in love with the music.

Richard was more on the administrative side. He didn't partake in the creative side because he was not musically inclined. Our younger brother Robert came into the business for a short time... he went to live in England but he never took too much interest in the music business.

My mother, Gloria Khouri, never produced records. She knew how to look after the money though! She was instrumental in building the business... dad was creative but mum knew more about the affordability that could go on! It was a company that was all fun and we had a great time! It was because of that that we progressed... we were always moving in harmony."
Paul Khouri

But, as Graeme Goodall had already proved, you did not have to be family, from Kingston or even from Jamaica to make music at Federal. Ken Khouri realised the importance of employing people who knew and understood, not only the recording business, but also the specific nuances of the Kingston musical scene as Paul Khouri later recounted.

Chapter 4

"Tom Dowd came after Graeme Goodall... he was the first. We were fortunate. We encountered people who kept the karma correct. Music cannot be created in turmoil. If you go in with the slightest hint of it...

'Buddy' Davidson was a wonderful engineer and a wonderful person. He was like family to us. He's now living in South Miami. A great engineer... wonderful... he worked with us for years. Buddy left in the exile in the Seventies... we couldn't fire him no more than I could fire myself! We had to have people like that who were one of us. It was a family affair. Buddy was working for the betterment of Federal and it was that way with all of us.

George Raymond was also an engineer. He overcame a struggle, learnt slowly and surely, and had a great understanding of what you would want. He was in love with creating something good in the sound... he was the most talented in doing what you wanted. You could depend on him!"
Paul Khouri

And Bunny 'Striker' Lee recalled the contribution made by recording engineer Al Iton:

"Federal were a record company and they had a two track studio for hire. Singer and band have to go same time and you had a great engineer there after Graeme Goodall left... He came from Barbados named Al Iton... he did more of the ska tunes. It's a pity someone didn't remember him or talk to him. He's an unsung hero... he did most of these Skatalites tunes with Duke Reid and Coxsone, Prince Buster all of them guys. He was one of the greatest engineers that came to Jamaica... he was not really a Jamaican. He and Graeme Goodall they used to be at Federal Studio. At that time you had two track recording. With most of them Skatalites things you had to record the horns man, the singers and everybody going at the same time so if a man made a mistake everything had to start over. Mr Iton was the engineer at the time... a lot of people don't even know him. He was a salesman too as the people at Federal used to sell records all around the Caribbean. Mr Iton was a gentleman but he was a great engineer and a great human being... he died the other day (December 2006)... Federal did have another engineer called 'Buddy' Davidson. He was a very good engineer who worked with Federal right through... and Paul Khouri became an engineer too."
Bunny 'Striker' Lee

And, as the music evolved, the musician's role became increasingly important but it was all too often undervalued for, while they were usually far more than just session musicians, their invaluable contributions, especially in the arrangement of the songs, were often overlooked. Throughout its entire development the Kingston music scene has evolved and revolved around these small, tight groups of session musicians who were instrumental in defining the direction of the music at any given time. Their names still remain all but unknown outside of people in the business and the few who avidly studied the small print on the back of a handful of LP sleeves.

"I think Jackie Jackson, all those musicians, they realised it's a recording industry and it became something like 'Well, we're part of it'. They started to experiment. Every one of them. The vocalist started to experiment, the producer started to… anything to get a little bit different. 'Cause remember they were virtually all the same session musicians for every single producer."
Graeme Goodall

But the role of the backing musicians appeared to be just that: to remain well in the background. But, without their prodigious skills, the records could never have been made. Needless to say there was no shortage of resentment from the musicians.

"It is usual for the producer to steal all of the limelight, and the money, for a record that he or she don't deserve any real praise for. Even though you might have had to compose a tune to fit an old rhythm track you still won't get any credit for it. You only get your normal session wages. Even if the singer gets some royalties the session man will not get anything."
Bobby Ellis

Federal Records employed their own in house band that included some of Kingston's greatest musicians.

"You've called all the names! They were there like forever! We didn't turn over our engineers… they were like family. Our in-house band included Paul Douglas on drums, Val Douglas on bass, Willie Lindo, Ernest Ranglin and Nerlyn 'Lynn' Taitt on guitars and Monty Alexander and Gladstone 'Gladdy' Anderson on piano. We had the greatest variety. We had Ernest Ranglin,

Monty Alexander, Lynn Taitt who came from Trinidad. We had Willie Lindo, too. We had local guys when we had use for them…"   **Paul Khouri**

As early as 1959 Ken Khouri had contracted jazz guitarist Ernest Ranglin as musical arranger at Federal. Responsible for arranging countless records for numerous nascent record producers Ernest Ranglin's crucial role still remains largely uncredited. One notable exception was Millie Small's cover of Barbie Gaye's 'My Boy Lollipop', recorded in the Pye four track studio in Marble Arch, London and released on Beverley's in Jamaica and on Fontana in the UK, which was uncharacteristically annotated 'Accompaniment Directed By Ernest Ranglin'. Recorded in London and produced by Chris Blackwell, 'My Boy Lollipop', was the first crossover ska hit reaching Number Two in the UK National Charts in early 1964. However, the musician's role usually meant keeping well out of sight if not out of hearing.

"They came to work regardless of whether they were recording or not… so when people came to make a record we could make a hit song immediately! It worked!"   **Paul Khouri**

Although rock steady only lasted for a very brief period its significance to the subsequent development of Jamaican music is incalculable. In 1966 the Trinidadian guitarist Nerlyn 'Lynn' Taitt, the acknowledged genius behind the next seismic shift in Jamaican music, was contracted to Federal Records. Derrick Morgan stated: "He's the man who changed Jamaican music right round from ska to rock steady". Many might have subsequently claimed to have put a halt to the rapid pace of ska by originating this new beat by recording the first rock steady record but, as always, the truth probably lies somewhere between the lines. Roy Shirley's story regarding his inspiration for 'Hold Them' for Joe Gibbs, which he recalled came from the sound of a Salvation Army marching band has, like the record itself, a particularly convincing authenticity. However, it is generally acknowledged that 'Take It Easy' by Hopeton Lewis, released on both the Federal and Merritone labels, and "recorded in the Federal Record Studios" was actually the very first. But Lynn Taitt did much more than slow the beat down: the manner in which he arranged the instruments with a constant melodic bass line defined the music that was to become known as 'reggae' throughout the world.

"For that tempo the tempo is very slow with the bass and guitar line playing the same thing. You used to use two guitars… Hux Brown and myself or another guitarist and myself... and it was very slow but with a definite bass line going straight through the song..." **Lynn Taitt**

The bass no longer gave equal emphasis to every beat but instead played a repeated pattern that syncopated the rhythm and the rhythmic focus shifted to the bass and the drums where it has remained ever since. The horn section, which been such a dominant feature of ska, was no longer so prominent and vocalists, influenced by American soul singers, now came into their own.

"Hopeton Lewis came to the Federal Recording Studio with a song called 'Take It Easy' and I find the ska was too fast. Very, very fast. So I told them let's do this one slow. Very slow. And as the music got slower it had spaces. The slower the music it have more spaces to do something with so I put a bass line and I play in unison with the bass and I get a bass line. And the piano, sometimes I strum, sometimes I play a bass line with the bass. That was the first slow song... nothing else was slow at that time. Everything had been ska" **Lynn Taitt**

Lynn Taitt was born 22nd June 1934 in San Fernando, Trinidad and began his musical career as a steel pan player and arranger when he was "eight or nine years old" and, at the age of fifteen, he acquired a guitar from a friend for twenty Trinidadian dollars and became a guitarist. At first he played his guitar in a group called The Dutch Brothers but after two years Lynn left to form his own group who were given a contract by Byron Lee in 1962 to go to Jamaica to play at the Independence celebrations. Lynn loved Jamaica so much that he decided to stay on and, after first joining The Sheiks, he moved on to The Cavaliers, performing at school dances and functions. He had already recorded as a guitarist with The Skatalites before forming Lynn Taitt & The Comets who started to do some recording in addition to their live dates and he established Lynn Taitt & The Jets in 1966. The group were signed to Federal Records on the strength of their leader's already formidable and musically forceful reputation. Credit must be given to piano player too, Gladstone 'Gladdy' Anderson, also a musical arranger for The Jets who had inadvertently given this new music a name on finishing the final take of 'Take It Easy' when he remarked on the 'rock steady' nature of the rhythm. One of his not so celebrated roles was as a translator for Lynn's Trinidadian accent.

Lynn Taitt

Richard Khouri and Ernest Ranglin at Federal Recording Studio

"I had a really strong Trinidadian accent...the Jamaicans didn't really understand it fully so Gladdy used to look after all of that. Talk to the singers and get everything clear." **Lynn Taitt**

Lynn was a modest and a self-deprecating man who, despite his all pervading influence referred to himself as "just an ordinary guitar player":

"It was a pleasure to get up and get an idea and put your idea on to a record and to have the public like what you do is a great gift. At the time we were not thinking of it from a business aspect. We were just interested in creating beautiful music... (I'm) just an ordinary guitar player trying to continue the heritage of black music from the West Indies." **Lynn Taitt**

"...then you'll realise that this guitarist is the party man who's been carrying the torch for the best sounds around town."
'Rock Steady Greatest Hits'

Paul Khouri also played on a number of Federal sessions...

"Then Hopeton Lewis and 'Take It Easy'. I played on all those rock steady albums... I played drums on Ernest Ranglin's 'Story Book Children'. I never wanted to be exposed and wasn't interested in propagating my name... just having a good time, having a ball and playing!"
Paul Khouri

Federal Records began to produce a series of some of the greatest ever rock steady releases for their Merritone subsidiary through an arrangement with one of the top sound systems in Jamaica run by Winston Blake.

"But we became very, very powerful... this little country sound became the talk of Kingston because we played a great variety of music... slow music, ballads. And people started to talk about us and our quality of sound. So instead of going to producers they now came to us... Duke Reid, Beverley's, Federal on Marcus Garvey Drive. If they only did three or four test presses we would always get a copy and at about midnight we'd say 'There's something new I'm going to break for you...' And we'd play it four or five times. Then they'd tell the radio stations! Our popularity grew and grew but we never competed with the hard core sound systems.

We had a production deal where Federal would use our name on the label. They did the productions and we would get a percentage of the profits. Lynn Taitt and Lloyd Charmers were major forces in the business at the time. I had a similar deal with Dynamics. I sat in on a lot of the sessions. I was the A&R man but I wasn't there when a lot of it was done... I was more of a consultant. I would get the test pressings and promote them. You had to make a decision on how many to press based on the crowd's reaction.

Merritone was like a brand name... once you saw it on the label you could compete with Treasure Isle and Studio One. The smart move that Federal made was that I would pay that brand much more attention! I did get some remuneration but we were all very young and very agreeable. We didn't think of money... we just wanted to be part of something that was working... part of the moment! The aura in the era worked well for Federal and very well for us also." **Winston 'Merritone' Blake**

The majority of the Merritone releases during 1967 and 1968 credited Sam Mitchell and Keith Scott on the label as producers and arrangers. Both men not only worked in the Federal pressing plant but, together with Winston Blake, also played an invaluable role in keeping the management at Federal on top of what was going on in the dance halls and on the sound systems.

"Sam Mitchell was a press man. He was a guy who worked in the factory and pressed records in the rock steady era with The Gaylettes etc but, because he lived downtown, he was a 'cricket'... a liaison role. He would come over and tell us how to link from one sector to another and would tell us if the music was right or wrong. We were making music for a different sector of society. Keith Scott was another press man and he did the same as Sam Mitchell." **Paul Khouri**

"It's a long story... I have to backtrack a bit! I was working at the Tropical Recording Company pressing plant with my friend Sam 'Mitch' Mitchell. It was owned by the Shakir family... they were Syrians... and they had the rights to press and distribute Imperial, Dot and Chess records in Jamaica. I worked for them from 1959 to 1960... I was just a kid. But in January 1961 we reported for work and the Tropical factory had burned down! I don't know what happened...

That February a friend of mine arranged with Ken Khouri, 'I know someone who has knowledge of the recording industry', and that's how I started. When I went into the factory Ken Khouri said to me 'you know the runnings?' and I said 'yes Mr Khouri'. We showed respect. The first thing I did was providing the pressing material... that's how I started... and I worked my way up to producing records in the Merritone era. My name was good and Winston Blake is absolutely correct...

When we started the tunes appeared on Federal and the sales were low! We had a meeting and no-one knew what the Federal label represented so Sam Mitchell said 'why don't we try to license Merritone's name?' and, before you know it, the sales for Merritone took off like wild fire. After that the label started getting popular and I worked at Federal until 1968... but we were young and inexperienced and we had a falling out with the Khouris. We left Federal and went to Byron Lee." **Keith 'Scotty' Scott**

One of the first Merritone releases, a major hit, came from The Tartans (Cedric Myton, Lloyd Robinson, Devon Russell and 'Prince' Lincoln Thompson) who recorded 'Dance All Night' for Federal and demonstrated exactly what could happen when the uptown 'society' elements who looked after the business came up against the downtown 'ghetto' sufferers who sang the hit songs. Roy Cousins, lead singer of The Royals, recalled how his group's first ever session at Federal Records, singing their own composition, 'House Upon The Hill', ended in disaster for the group. The tape remained in the Federal vaults until it was discovered by Naoki lenaga, of Dub Store in Japan, who released it some fifty years later. Roy Cousins takes up the story.

"'Cause even 'House Upon The Hill' it's a rough take so you can imagine if we go back and do it again we'd do it far, far better. It's not properly voiced. We just stood round the piano player, sing along, and he'd get the chords. When he got it together he'd set up two microphones but it was just us singing round the piano.

It was Prince Lincoln who broke the session up... some big argument. We used to play football down the bottom of Cling Cling Avenue and there were two notorious gangs in the area... the Pigeon and the Sweetest. What happened was we all used to rehearse together... Harry (Berthram Johnson) was the only one in the area with a guitar and The Tartans went to the Federal audition before we and they got selected and made their hit 'Dance All Night'... the lyrics 'do the sweetest dance' was for the Sweetest gang... but it was we who actually rehearsed the track. We did all the ground work for it... we used to sing by timing: one, two, three, four then sing. The Tartans came up to our yard because of Berthram's guitar.

You had to be lucky to pass one of these auditions so it make sense to make it right... you had to be well, well, well rehearsed. When we finally went to Federal and got selected the day when we were doing the track Prince Lincoln and Devon Russell claimed that 'House Upon The Hill' was too similar to 'Dance All Night' and bring this notorious gang from Cockburn Pen and Waterhouse to stop the session... they were some dangerous men... and mayhem was created when we were inside singing that track. For what? Just to stop we from getting a break... this is to show you the extreme these guys would go to. That's why I can't remember... we were singing and murder was going on outside.

Ken Khouri, the father, came in and said 'stop the session' and asked us to leave. He gave The Tartans priority because they were already with them and had a hit. And Trevor McFarlane, the man who sang lead on 'House Upon The Hill'... Cedric Myton is married to his sister... Trevor walked away and said he would never ever sing again and, true enough, Trevor never ever sang again. Gladstone 'Gladdy' Anderson was the one who played the piano and he said to us we were to come down to Treasure Isle on Sunday... come to audition 'cause he was the one who did the auditions for Duke Reid." **Roy Cousins**

Despite these setbacks, and by simultaneously looking at the bigger picture, Federal were later able to insinuate the sound of rock steady into the heights of the UK National Charts. 'Hold Me Tight', a record that paired Johnny Nash (born August 19th 1940 in Houston, Texas, USA) with a beautiful Lynn Taitt rock steady arrangement, reached Number Five in the UK National Charts in August 1968 where it was released on Regal Zonophone. Produced at the Federal studios by Johnny Nash, Arthur Jenkins and Paul Khouri and arranged and conducted by Arthur Jenkins and Lynn Taitt the record has rarely been given the credit its early crossover success deserves... perhaps because it was performed by a well known American singer. 'Hold Me Tight' backed by an update of Sam Cooke's 'Cupid', reputedly sold six million copies on the international market and

Chapter 4

The Royals (left to right): Roy Cousins, Berthram 'Harry' Johnson, Errol Wilson/Nelson, Keith 'Super' Smith

Johnny Nash recorded a French language version, 'Reviens Moi', over the original rhythm for the Canadian market. Bunny 'Striker' Lee recalled how Federal were, at first, unable to keep up with the unprecedented demand in the UK and the amusing outcome.

"Reggae brought back Johnny Nash with 'Hold Me Tight'... Lynn Taitt did play it, you know. When it was first coming to England it was coming up on pre but Federal wasn't putting it out fast enough and the people really wanted it so this man just cut it and started pirating it and selling 'Hold Me Tight' and 'Cupid' on white label... it wasn't on no label. Then Johnny Nash came to Jamaica and said 'Show me the man that put out the tune! I'd like to meet this guy'. Instead of Johnny Nash being vexed with him he took his hand and gave him five hundred pounds and said 'Buy a drink! Thank you, man, for promoting me in England!' Yeah! Him pirate the tune and Johnny Nash gave him five hundred pounds!"

Bunny 'Striker' Lee

A number of American artists travelled to Kingston to record at Federal but Johnny Nash was one of the few who actually wholeheartedly embraced Jamaican music. 'You Got Soul' was another UK Top Ten hit the following year and his 1972 cover of 'Stir It Up' was the first crossover hit for a young songwriter named Bob Marley. Paul Khouri recalled the hard work that went into making 'Hold Me Tight'. "... Then we also had a lot of involvement with foreign musicians coming down here like Johnny Nash with his entire band. He did a lot of sounds at Federal. 'Hold Me Tight' with Johnny Nash? I lost my girlfriend on the beach over that song! But that's what the music has to come back to... As a matter of fact Marvin Gaye recorded in our studio. There were many major artists that everybody knew who spent a lot of time with us. Paul Anka was one... but I cannot remember all of their names."

Paul Khouri

Federal continued to expand its critical role in the development of Jamaican music and became known as "the centre of Jamaica's music business". Innumerable 'local' records were recorded, mastered and pressed at Marcus Garvey Drive. They also released a number of albums in America on their Steady subsidiary label, 'Solid Gold: Reggae's Greatest Hits', that echoed Trojan's 'Tighten Up' series in the UK.

"Federal Records opened this bigger studio. I mean it just got completely out of hand and, wonder of wonders, we had a separate disc cutting room. We also made our own stampers... We started off this mono, then two track then three track. With the new studio I used to put the vocal separate and they said let's do the b side without the vocal... so the deejays used to speak along with it and crack rhymes.

Later when I was recording in stereo I would often record a backing track or whatever and this became the b side or the dub side. You know, these guys would cut four songs probably on one ten inch acetate, 45 rpm, then when they got that out they would press it on blank and they would sell that for maybe five times the amount of a single. Again, this is not only to sound systems, but also to juke box operators, people like that."

Graeme Goodall

"Well there was no record company in the world like Federal. We were the only one, and I say this very proudly, that we could go into the studio in the morning at eight o'clock for recording, and on the same day at five o'clock finished product was on the street. We had the facilities to record and master, make stampers and press records, print labels and jackets. We had our own art department and we had our own photo studio. Every department needed in the music industry was in five or six acres of Federal facilities from Marcus Garvey Drive right up to Bell Road. We did not need to go out to do anything. Around 1968 or 1969 someone had tried to burn our studio down because we were putting so much pressure on the industry. You know, hits after hits, all the time. We were making so many powerful hit records. So that was the only way they thought they could stop us. And they did stop us for about a year. Meantime, we got an acoustic engineer from England called Derrick Softing. We designed our new studio. We bought a Neve console from England, MCI sixteen track tape recorder, Yamaha nine foot grand piano, Hammond organ, all that stuff. So we kept going..."

Paul Khouri

"I did a lot of work at Federal too... Bob Andy do 'Games People Play' and a lot of my personal tunes were made at Federal Studios. Rhythms like 'Ain't Too Proud To Beg' with Slim Smith, 'Slip Away' with Slim Smith. I gave Scratch a cut of it. He put Dave Barker on it... 'Prisoner Of Love' Dave Barker sing on it. 'Kiss Me Each Morning' ('If It Don't Work Out') with Pat Kelly... all of those tunes were made at Federal Studio. Variety is the spice

of life... you don't have one sound. You understand? But tunes like 'How Long' by Pat Kelly were made at Dynamics on the home ground."
Bunny 'Striker' Lee

And, despite manufacturing and mastering slowing down considerably in 1970 due to the fire, it was business as usual and, as the decade progressed, Federal continued to cater for the 'local' market and also concentrated on keeping ahead of all the latest technological developments.

"In those days reggae was like a throwaway thing... the records come this week and the people don't want last week's records. So you could press twenty five or fifty records at Federal and, if you sell them, you could go back and press twenty five or fifty more. Me came into the business by booking an hour studio time... then two hours. Tado (Dr Alimantado) told me he started by booking half an hour..." **Roy Cousins**

"He (Ken Khouri) always went to the USA because he was involved with labels like Mercury, Capitol and so on. So he went to their technical side in the studios to get advanced knowledge about the technology. You know, every year fresh technology came up just like now and we were motivated by the technology more than money. When our generation came I tried the same... so did my brother Richard Khouri. We made contacts in the business all over the world to get new and fresh technology: people like Louis 'Buddy' Davidson pushed us forward... a wonderful engineer. A wonderful person. He was like family to us. He's now living in South Miami. A great engineer... wonderful... he worked with us for years. Federal Records was way ahead of everybody in the business." **Paul Khouri**

Their state of the art equipment was matched by the quality of their productions and Federal enjoyed great success throughout the Caribbean with vocalist Ken Lazarus who had previously sung with Byron Lee & The Dragonaires. Paul Khouri recounted with great humour how they could have enjoyed even greater success with an artist named Hugh Faulkner had it not been for his jealous wife.

"Ken Lazarus was very popular in the islands. He made the BBC News in Guyana in 1971 or 1972! Ken Lazarus dominated the top ten charts. Check the BBC log from those years! Ken Lazarus took up the top ten places in the top ten! We also had the number one singer in Brazil... Hugh Faulkner. Andy

Williams, Quincy Jones and Henry Mancini were all the judges and they voted Hugh Faulkner as the number one singer! He was an East Indian gentleman and his wife got very jealous. CBS, RCA all came with deals for him but he disappeared for five years. His wife took him and hid him away! We thought he'd died. When he came back we had to tell him 'It's too late! You're forgotten now. You're no longer a star!'" **Paul Khouri**

But during the Seventies Federal's polished perfection came to be regarded in some quarters as being out of step with the overwhelming rise of roots music. Some contemporary critics were able to see the value of the music while others saw Federal's clear, crisp perfection as the antithesis of what reggae music was now perceived to be all about:

"You can always count on a Federal record to give you something that's well sung, well played and well produced…" **Chris Lane**

"Federal, a home of well groomed and mildly ambitious singers and musicians who produce refined Jamaican music, lightweight material… believing it is the brand of reggae the whole world should hear. Reggae that is correct and clean." **Carl Gayle**

As ever the record buying public saw things their own way and Ken Boothe's interpretation of David Gates' 'Everything I Own', produced by Lloyd Charmers for Federal, became a resounding Number One hit on the UK National Charts in September 1974.

"Lloyd Charmers never actually worked at Federal… we created a label for him with fifty/fifty ownership of production and he got paid according to the agreement. He came into Federal Records in 1972 or 1973. His records were released on Wild Flower but our productions were released on the label too. Derrick Harriott, Lloyd Charmers and other producers all wanted to join up with Federal as we had the golden touch… we did it right for the people." **Paul Khouri**

Paul Khouri also produced a series of international crossover hits with 'Pluto' Shervington, originally released on Wild Flower in Jamaica, that comprised a bit of roots, a bit of pop and a great deal of good humour. These records took a while to cross over into the general public's consciousness and it is doubtful that many of the consumers who purchased 'Dat' in the UK, credited to Pluto and first released in Jamaica in 1974, knew what the song was all about: an amusing tale about a struggling Rastafarian's attempts to hide that fact he is unable to afford anything to eat but pork so "to protect the humble we change the name". The jaunty rhythm, Pluto's pleading and the butcher's (played to perfection by bassist Lloyd Parks) insouciant delivery propelled 'Dat', now on the Opal label, to Number Six in the UK National Charts in February 1976. 'Ram Goat Liver' was also originally released in 1974 and reached the lower regions of the UK Chart National Chart (Number 43) in April 1976 when Trojan released it in the wake of 'Dat'. 'Your Honour', from 1975, then took seven years to climb the charts and was a seriously belated Number 19 hit in the UK in March 1982 where it was issued on the KR label. Paul Khouri remained characteristically modest.

"Pluto Shervington... Ernie Smith... in Japan we had the number one song with Ernie Smith 'Life Is For Living' but I was not trying to overshadow the artists. I produced but the propagation was all about the artists."

Paul Khouri

On the rare occasions that Federal did venture into the roots market, through licensing or pressing and distribution deals, the results were never less than excellent. U Roy's 'Foundation Skank' backed by a staggering King Tubby's style deconstruction of 'Sweet Talking', The Abyssinians' 'Reason Time' and Errol Dunkley's 'One Love' were all released on Federal's Rebel subsidiary and number, respectively, among the best ever recordings from the 'deejay daddy', one of the greatest of Jamaica's vocal groups and one of its most accomplished singers.

But the Khouri family found themselves increasingly out of step, not only musically, but also with the political climate of the times. The Jamaican experiment in democratic socialism conducted by Prime Minister Michael Manley's PNP (People's National Party) and the close links Michael Manley was forging with near neighbour Fidel Castro's communist regime in Cuba convinced a number of Jamaica's upper and middle classes that Jamaica's very own people's revolution was imminent. Many emigrated to Florida, USA to escape the cataclysm that they were certain was fast approaching.

"Unfortunately we got 'the scare'... the political problem... so we moved all the equipment out otherwise we thought they might have taken it away from us. We were naïve people and very insular, we could not see further than our

Chapter 4

noses, so we were panicked. I think we panicked a little bit more than necessary but that is something you cannot reverse. That was something we had to accept. I left, and so did my brother, but my parents could not leave because they were old. Buddy Davidson also left in the exile in the Seventies... I couldn't fire Buddy no more than I could fire myself! We had to have people like that who were one of us. It was a family affair. Buddy was working for the betterment of Federal and it was that way with all of us and that's what made it so difficult when we left Jamaica...." **Paul Khouri**

And, after setting up KK Mastering in Miami, Florida Paul Khouri had to struggle to make it a success and survive. The wealth and depth of experience he had built up in Jamaica now meant little in the USA and he had to work for next to nothing in order to establish his credentials.

"Then I started my own label. My legal name is Kenneth and my middle name is Paul and I'm known as Paul but for the mastering labs I kept Kenneth for me and Kenneth for my father... so KK Mastering. I was a mastering engineer and, in the Seventies exodus, we sneaked out the equipment in a container by saying it was 'personal effects'. We were based at 1986 North East 149th Street in Miami and we suffered for many years. 'Who the hell is this Jamaican engineer compared to Criteria Recording Studio?' They were four hundred yards down the road. So I had to pay my dues. It was expensive in terms of my energy. Eckhardt Krieger and I were like best friends. He stayed with me in Florida and left the equipment. I went over to Criteria and, as it was the only way to let them see what I was capable of, I worked for free. I told them I'd keep the tape heads aligned as the azimuth would go out of alignment... but the only way to get a job was to do it for free. Their machines were in sh*t condition and I'd get a $10 tip for working from seven at night to five in the morning and, eventually, they got to find out that I knew what I was doing."
Paul Khouri

Paul eventually found his feet and, together with vocalist Eddie Lovette, went on to produce two of the biggest selling reggae albums of the Eighties: 'Rockers For Lovers Volumes 1 & 2'. These smooth, mellow albums were the sophisticated epitome of what was known in the business as 'Big People's Music'. Paul takes up the story.

"I owe my wife 50% of everything I've done because of her confidence in me! I got jobs to cut records but it wasn't enough to keep me going. She was pregnant at the time with our third daughter and she said 'let's go out for a night of relaxation'. We went out to Le Jardin... Chuck Mangione (American flugel horn player and composer) and his brother Trip Mangione owned the club. There was no cover charge and when he took a break Eddie Lovette came on stage... I knew him from Jamaica. The first song Eddie and I recorded was a version of The Commodores' 'Sail On'. It sold about 170,000 copies in Miami and down in the islands. We were getting samples two or three weeks prior to release and we received The Manhattans' 'Shining Star'... so our version came out first. We were pressing twenty four hours round the clock! At this stage I never had the time or the energy to go back and help out at the other studios. They rang me up and said 'We'll pay you!' If I had had the energy I would have done it but I would have burnt myself to the ground. 'I'm tired. I'm sorry...' I produced Eddie Lovette from 1979 to 1989. Another wonderful ten years! He won the International Artist Award in Canada. We'd only prepared one track and he sung the first track with the backing and the second in acapella... a very difficult song... and the people stood up and screamed! There was no greater moment than that! Although I wasn't singing I had the thrill of knowing I was a part of it. Afterwards he had a hard time getting rid of people but I had no problem! He had a warm time... signing and signing! Why would I want to suffer like that?" **Paul Khouri**

Although the recording equipment had been shipped to Miami the company continued custom pressing records for the local producers and Federal also exported records to the other Caribbean islands, the USA and the UK.

"But Federal never closed. Federal operated without the recording equipment. We could not move the pressing plant. It was impossible. We operated the business until the early Eighties." **Paul Khouri**

"Richard Khouri did sell it out... They couldn't get enough vinyl to press the records... politics was involved... so they just sell out the company. Vinyl was what carried at the time and the oil prices gone up and vinyl was getting short and they're not getting the licence in time to clear it so they couldn't keep up with the custom pressing. So they just sell out." **Bunny 'Striker' Lee**

"Also, my parents could not keep up with the pace of the record industry. They recognised that I was not coming back as I was successful in the States. So they decided to sell up Federal and retire." **Paul Khouri**

However, Paul Khouri had few regrets...

"Today's music is so revolutionary and war like. There's no more love. No more smile. We would laugh from the start of the session to the end. We were laughing throughout and it all came out in the music. We were just having a ball... People can enjoy many different types of music... but seventy versions of the same track! They're squeezing the last juice out of the orange. The digital world has taken the human feeling out of the sound. We used to record analogue and convert to digital. But it's taken the human feel out of it... a little imperfection is only human! I believe it's taken a lot away. People want the old records again... I guess that's what we call progression!" **Paul Khouri**

After Bob Marley's untimely death in May 1981 Rita Marley took over the running of the Tuff Gong organisation and purchased Federal Records later that year.

"I sold the studio and pressing plant to Tuff Gong, Bob Marley's company, in 1981 but I'm proud of everything as the music business was something that I loved. I know that I used to keep stepping up and up and up with everything modern, keep improving till I had everything I wanted." **Ken Khouri**

"They eventually bought everything so it became Tuff Gong Music... but we did not sell our Federal catalogue to Tuff Gong." **Paul Khouri**

Paul Khouri recalled that Bob Marley had recorded for Federal at the start of his career but, out of respect for Bob's legacy, he later destroyed the tapes. Wailers' fans might well eat their hearts out at the thought of this but it is a measure of Paul Khouri's integrity that he decided to do so rather than exploit the memory of a man he considered to be good friend.

"Without Federal there would have been no Bob Marley! I had a lot of tapes of Bob in his infancy. He came to us with no shoes... I burnt the tapes because it would have been a deterrent to a good friend. They were not ready for release. It could have destroyed a person and why would I do that? I'm an artist and I'm not going to destroy someone artistically for a couple of pennies. It's not my style. I knew Bob very well... I grew up with him..." **Paul Khouri**

Possibly the small axe was finally cutting down at least one of the big trees or perhaps Bob appreciated Federal's place in the history of Jamaican music and Ken Khouri's crucial role.

"My dad never believed in self praise. He would despise anyone who would stand up and say 'I am…' or 'I was…'. He did not do it all, you know. He created the highway to drive high speed on and people capitalised on it. He had to have a lot of courage to believe in himself to start something new like that and have it grow. But very few people have credited him or recognised the background… Bob Marley did.

The only other man who has personally acknowledged to me my dad's involvement was Chris Blackwell from Island Records. Chris told me that my dad had made it really truly possible for all of us to be what we are today. I do not think he himself believed that he could have brought it to where he brought it though. He lived his life knowing what he had achieved and was very content. And he was very proud of the record industry of the Jamaican people today, you know, how they are taking it on. They expose themselves to the world." **Paul Khouri**

Richard and Paul Khouri, together with their families, returned to reside in Jamaica in the early Eighties and Paul recalled "I wasn't happy in Florida even though I was making more money than I'd ever made in my life. I couldn't live in Florida." In 2001 Ken Khouri was inducted into the Hall of Fame of the Caribbean Development for the Arts and Culture Foundation, in August 2003 he was belatedly honoured at Kingston's annual Tributes To The Greats ceremony and in September the Institute Of Jamaica Historical Society awarded Ken Khouri its Musgrave medal. But his inestimable contribution to the development of the Jamaican music industry has never been officially recognised and he has yet to recieve an accolade from the Jamaican Government. Ken Khouri died on 20th September 2003 in Kingston at the age of 86.

"My old man… he was the creator. He made it all possible and he died without the recognition. I asked him 'Dad. Why don't you write a book?' and he replied 'That's your choice Paul. Look how happy we are. Do I need this out there to tell people who I am? We knew what we had done. What's the purpose of it all? But I'm not fighting recognition. I've had a wonderful life, a wonderful time and I wouldn't change anything for the world. I'm happy I went through all these times…" **Paul Khouri**

In our lengthy interview Paul Khouri told the story of Federal Records with love and affection and without a hint of rancour. We hope, in some small way, that this chapter will help towards gaining some long overdue recognition for the amazing achievements of Federal Records.

"It was his Federal Recording Studio, the womb that gave birth to the talented writers, artists and musicians, that gave Jamaica its musical identity."
Prince Buster

Records Ltd, 129 King Street, Kingston

Producer:
Ken Khouri

Labels:
Capitol, Kalypso & Times Record

Federal Record Manufacturing
220 Foreshore Road
Hagley Park PO
Kingston

Federal Record Manufacturing Company Ltd
220 Marcus Garvey Drive
Kingston 11

Producers:
Ken Khouri & Paul Khouri

Engineers include:
Louis 'Buddy' Davidson, Tom Dowd, Graeme Goodall, Al Iton, Paul Khouri, Ken Khouri, Richard Khouri, George Raymond & Byron 'Baron'/'Smithy' Smith

Labels:
Federal, FRM, LTD, Merritone, Rebel, Steady, The Turntable & Wild Flower

Musicians:
Lynn Taitt & The Jets:
Bass: Bryan Atkinson
Drums: Joe Isaacs
Guitars: Lynn Taitt & Hux Brown
Piano: Gladstone 'Gladdy' Anderson & Theophilus 'Easy Snappin'' 'Beckford

Chapter 5

Noel Hawks

Chapter 5
Dancing To The Music Of Sir Coxsone The Downbeat Studio One

"The importance of Studio One music to the Jamaican music industry cannot be over stressed. Without Clement Dodd's progressive thinking in the blues dominated late Fifties the Jamaican music scene may well have stagnated without having the opportunity to change from imitation American rhythm & blues to ska which was to become known worldwide as Jamaica's new national music…"   **Chris Lane**

Clement Seymour 'Coxsone' Dodd was the first sound system operator to open his own recording studio, Studio One, and over the ensuing years the names Coxsone and Studio One have become synonymous with reggae. It is automatically assumed that every classic Jamaican 'oldie' must come from Studio One and that the original of any 'do-over' rhythm currently doing the dance hall rounds must also emanate from the same source. The pre-eminence of Studio One in the history of Jamaican music is a direct result of Coxsone's musical intelligence and business acumen. His ability to see further than whatever the current styles and fashions in music happened to be has assured his prominent position in the history of reggae and, as well as producing and pressing new records, a superb selection of oldies was always readily available in Mr Dodd's record shops.

"...and being a collector of oldies I would often times become very frustrated and disappointed because I could not purchase the record anywhere." **Clement 'Coxsone' Dodd**

Renowned as a training ground for new talent practically every artist and musician of note in the story of Jamaican music began their apprenticeship at Brentford Road and Studio One boasts a catalogue that constitutes a complete history of Jamaican music. This might sound like hyperbole, most producers "have their time" but little longevity, yet no other record producer, studio or label comes close to emulating the remarkable achievements of Studio One.

Clement Seymour Dodd was born 26th January 1932 in Kingston, Jamaica the son of Benjamin Dodd, a building contractor and mason who had helped build the Carib Theatre, and Doris Darlington after whom he would later name his D Darling label. He spent some of his formative years in the rural parish of St. Thomas where, at All Saints School, he allegedly acquired his nickname due to his prowess on the cricket field although some stories suggest a more risqué origin of this soubriquet. 'Coxsone' was supposedly taken from the Yorkshire opening bowler Alec Coxon while other sources have suggested that the name came from Bill Copson who bowled for the neighbouring county of Derbyshire.

"During the West Indians' tour of England in 1939 Copson routed them twice: he took ten wickets for Derbyshire v West Indies followed by nine wickets for England v West Indies at Lord's just a few weeks later."

His influence on Jamaican music would prove to be profound but he was not a musician and Coxsone was a cabinet maker by trade. His first encounter with the music business was the purchase of a Morphy Richards radio and an extension speaker to play his Louis Jordan and Billy Eckstine records to the customers at his mother's restaurant, 'Nanny's Corner', at the downtown junction of Laws Street and Ladd Lane in Kingston. He continued to entertain Mrs Darlington's patrons when she relocated the restaurant to the corner of Beeston Street and Love Lane.

"Mrs Darlington was married to a man that Sir Alexander Bustamante did kick and he did get famous through that... she named Darlington but Coxsone's father was named Dodd... him and the mother ran some liquor

stores too. One was off the Waltham Park Road and one I don't quite remember if it's Beeston Street and… Luke Lane? Love Lane? Yeah. Love Lane. I think so. It's where the sound started from…"
Bunny 'Striker' Lee

Coxsone's parents were friendly with Arthur 'Duke' Reid who supplied their business with beer, wine and spirits from his Treasure Isle Liquor Store and the Duke would sometimes allow Coxsone to play guest spots on his sound system.

"Duke Reid's Sound was before Coxsone. Coxsone's mother, whose married name was Miss Darlington, was friendly with Duke Reid. Duke Reid set up Doris Darlington in the liquor business… you could say she was the first woman deejay."
Bunny 'Striker' Lee

"After leaving school Coxsone had signed a farm work contract which took him to the southern USA as a sugarcane cutter. It was there, after work, that he first heard the music that he soon came to love and Coxsone soon became a connoisseur."
Steve Barrow

And, while working in the ranks of Jamaican migrant labour in Florida, Coxsone sent home a box of records, a turntable, a Bogan amplifier and some speakers to his mother who had boxes for the speakers built to his specifications. Miss Darlington played the inaugural session, "actually the first session it was my mother operated the sound system" with this equipment.

"Coxsone was away on farm work because Coxsone was a cabinet maker before the music business… So Coxsone started off Miss Darlington with a little sound and she used to play it. So when Coxsone came back from farm work he found his mother playing the little sound and she started to sell liquor. Duke set her up in the liquor store because Duke Reid was a man with a big liquor store so Miss Darlington made good use of it… because if you good at farm work the farmer would take you back every year so he started bringing in rhythm & blues records just like Duke."
Bunny 'Striker' Lee

"Whilst in America he first heard the music that he soon came to love… principally the new rhythm & blues but also including the bluesier side of

bebop. This music was the choice of the urban black working class who had migrated to the large cities during the war years; by the end of the Forties it had supplanted the pre-war swing, jive and blues styles."
Steve Barrow

On his return to Jamaica towards the end of 1954 Coxsone established his sound system 'Sir Coxsone The Downbeat' which was built by an associate of Hedley Jones named Jack Eastwood. This would eventually expand to five different 'Sir Coxsone The Downbeat' sets featuring legendary deejay figures such as Michael 'Count Matchuki' Cooper, who had previously deejayed for Tom Wong and Winston 'King Stitt The Ugly One' Sparkes. Cecil Bustamente Campbell, better known as Prince Buster, was an early employee on the sound.

"Prince Buster, leader of an informal street gang based around Charles Street in downtown Kingston initially stepped in to provide Coxsone with security for his dances, on at least one occasion defending Dodd by intervening physically. So Buster became another member of the Coxsone team... he also ensured that the set attracted a large number of patrons to their dances." **Steve Barrow**

> Sound System Amplifier, 120 watt and 60 watt and speakers New and old blues records Apply Coxson's Down Beat 45 Mark Lane

"Duke Reid the Trojan had the sound of the day. He has the strength of money and equipment. But Coxsone had records and exclusive selecting."
Count Matchuki

When Coxsone began to produce his own records he enrolled master musicians such as Aubrey Adams, Roland Alphonso (a childhood friend) and Cluett 'Clue J' Johnson. At first he used the recording and pressing facilities at Ken Khouri's Federal Records and 'Shuffling Jug', credited to Clue J & His Blues Busters, recorded at Federal in 1956 and eventually released on Coxsone's Worldisc label, is generally acknowledged to be the first CS Dodd production.

"At his first session in Federal Studio in 1956 Coxsone recorded Cluett Johnson & His Blues Busters on a boogie version of the Glenn Miller swing hit, 'Little Brown Jug' from 1939.(The tune was built around a drinking song from 1869). Coxsone called his version 'Shuffling Jug' and this recording was initially only for sound system use. Both Coxsone and tenor saxophonist Roland Alphonso were admirers of Glenn Miller's tenor player, Tex Beneke." **Steve Barrow**

At first Coxsone also used the facilities at the short lived Tropical Recording Company which burned down in early 1961. This small pressing plant and recording studio, which had a licence to press American records including Imperial, Dot and Chess, was owned and run by the Shakir family. The first Jamaican record producers rarely produced the records themselves, in the previously accepted sense of the term, and employed accomplished jazz and dance band musicians to create the type of music that they wanted to play on their sets.

"Coxsone came and asked me if I would do some local recordings for him. I never really thought about it as I was really concentrating on the jazz scene." **Tommy McCook**

Wholly immersed in Jamaican rhythm & blues sound system culture these pioneers initially aimed only to please other aficionados and improve their status within it. The links between the producer and the audience were both very close and very real: music recorded in the afternoon could be cut on to acetates and played the same night to test the audience reaction.

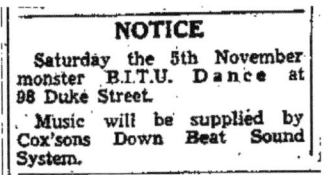

"I was dancing to the music of Sir Coxsone The Downbeat on the beach..."
'On The Beach' Owen Gray

The impact of hearing Owen Gray extolling the virtues of Dodd's Sound System playing out at a dance must have been indescribably exciting. Owen takes up the story:

Chapter 5

"They used to have sound system dances on the North Coast in Mobay (Montego Bay) and Ochi (Ocho Rios). King Edwards was playing at Ochi and I went to the dance with The Blues Busters... I sat on a rock, viewing the young girls in their beach outfits and the waves were coming so I rolled up my trousers and paddled a little, tried to chat up a couple of the girls and just listened and danced to the music. The sound was playing '3 x 7 = 21' by Dave Bartholomew then you have one like 'South Fork, West Virginia' by Louis Jordan and then this rhythm came on... 'dum, dum, dum, dum...' (sings) and I went up to the guy and I asked him 'Have you got a piece of paper?' I was never without a pencil... you can always sharpen a pencil... and he gave me a pamphlet (what we now call a flyer) and I just started writing 'I saw females on the beach one Sunday morning and I was jumping to the sound system' and I went up to the guy again... and asked him to play back the rhythm because I'm going to sing a song.

He said 'You can sing little boy?' and he turned to the next deejay. So I said to him 'What's the name of the sound?' and he said 'You can read? It's on the front of the speaker box... King Edwards' and then he said 'Gather round, gather round and listen to the little youth' and all the girls came to the front. He said 'You ready?' and gave me the mic. and this feedback started so he told me to hold the mic. away. I started 'I was dancing to the music of King Edwards The Giant on the beach'... I sung it three or four times. On the Monday I went to see King Edwards in Kingston and he said 'I hear you sing a song about the sound? Sing it make me hear it.' So I did and he said 'It sound good. Meet me Thursday at Federal Records down on Foreshore Road'.

But every time I went to see him there he turned me down so I went downtown... hopped a truck... and came off at Orange Street, up King Street and up Love Lane towards Charles Street. I saw Coxsone coming down... I never knew him but my Dad did... so I said 'I'm looking for Mr Coxsone'. He had a bar down Love Lane and some little houses he used to rent to people. There was one with a printing machine... I had learned printing and bookbinding... I saw a piano in the other room and he asked me 'Do you know how to play?' and he gave me a soft drink... a bottle of Fanta. I said 'I have written a song about your sound system' and I played it on the piano and sang at the same time. He stopped me and said 'Hold on... don't let nobody hear you sing any more!'"

He 'phoned his mum and she came down so I said 'Hello Mrs Dodd'... I always have respect for the Dodd family. He said 'Play it again. What's your name?' and she turned to Coxsone and said 'Take him to the studio... Roland (Alphonso) is coming down tomorrow'. And he said 'Where do you live?' and he dropped me home in his black Buick. Coxsone never changed his car. I think it's still around... parked in the studio. But when my mum saw me in the car she thought something bad had happened! Coxsone said 'You have a star here... didn't you know? I'm coming for him tomorrow to do something'.

The engineer at Federal studio was Graeme Goodall... everything was live, live, live... no coming back next week! Roland was there in the studio... Arkland 'Drumbago' Parks on drums, Lloyd Brevett on bass, Roland Alphonso on tenor saxophone, Lester Sterling on alto saxophone, Don Drummond on trombone... it was Don Drummond's first recording session... Lester Sterling took a part of the solo and he took the second part... Herman Hersang was on piano and Jerome 'Jah Jerry' Hines was the guitarist. Before they started recording Roland said 'Run it over... Listen to the youth. He has a bad... I don't want to cuss no bad words in front of the youth... tune'. So they set up the mic. and then the rhythm start... one lick you know. This was a Wednesday and King Stitt played it on the sound that night. Then everywhere I went I heard the tune when Downbeat used to play. He used to play 'On The Beach' against King Edwards and, when I saw him, I had to say 'but you didn't want the tune... you said come back the next day and the next day and the next day'..." **Owen Gray**

After extensive, exclusive play throughout 1959 on Downbeat sound 'On The Beach' was eventually released in 1960 on Coxsone's Cariboo label where the all star band were credited as The Coxsonairs. Two years later it was released in London on Emil E Shallit's Dice subsidiary label where it was erroneously credited as 'A Buster's Recording' by Owen Gray and Buster's Group.

"'On The Beach' was recorded in 1959 and was the first Jamaican record to mention a sound system by name... he recorded it for Sir Coxsone Downbeat and cut a 'special', designed exclusively for sound system use, but it proved popular enough to warrant release to the public at large when Coxsone **Steve Barrow**

If there was a favourable response to the reference disc then a seven inch vinyl white blank label 'pre-release' would be issued in a limited pressing selling for fifteen shillings (seventy five pence) more than twice the price of a standard release. It was usually only other sound system operators and juke box owners who could afford to purchase these advance copies which helped to promote the record, build up the demand and pave the way for an eventual release. No market research surveys were required: the music was made by people who were part of the audience directly for that same audience. It harboured no pretensions or intentions to reach outside of its immediate target audience and no-one was considering the possible 'crossover' market or any form of international success.

"I didn't realise that this could be a business! I just did it for enjoyment!"
Clement 'Coxsone' Dodd

Towards the end of 1959 Coxsone opened his first Muzik City record shop on East Queen Street and travelled throughout the USA looking for records, firstly to play on his sound, secondly to sell to other sound systems and then to customers in his record shop.

"New York, Chicago, Philadelphia and Cincinnati to find more and more exclusive tunes. Rainbow Records on 130th Street in Harlem, New York proved to be a lucrative source of good music and he was lucky enough to find a wealth of records in Brooklyn." **Rob Chapman**

"Now when we were buying records from America for Jamaica these were old records. These weren't current records…"
Clement 'Coxsone' Dodd

He then opened Coxon's Dramatic & Music Centre at 67½ Church Street (entrance in Love Lane) and, as the business continued to grow, he moved to 136D Orange Street in 1963 and later opened another shop at 10 Cumberland Road in Spanish Town.

"Coxsone's shop was on Orange Street…" **Bunny 'Striker' Lee**

We had a retail outlet on Orange Street for a number of years, another outlet on Bedford Street in the market area and another store on East Queen Street." **Clement 'Coxsone' Dodd**

Instead of relying on increasingly scarce American rhythm & blues records, Coxsone started to record, sell and distribute his own productions on a bewildering variety of labels including All Stars, Cariboo, Coxsone, C and N, D Darling, Cariboo, Muzik City, ND Records, Rolando & Powie, Supreme and Worldisc. These productions had a vitality and an edge that transformed them into something very special and his fierce, single minded independence proved pivital to the music transcending its 'local' beginnings.

Lee Perry also numbered among Coxsone's early employees and they started working together after Coxsone had noticed him at a Duke Reid session in the Federal studio. At first he was a talent scout and ran auditions but began to make his own vocal records, including 'Chicken Scratch' where he acquired his 'Scratch' epithet, and he would also contribute percussion on sessions. In 1962 he worked on a series of records aimed specifically at rival sound systems, including former Coxsone employee Prince Buster, with a young Delroy Wilson who recounted to writer Steve Barrow in 1994:

"It was like Prince Buster against Coxsone against Duke Reid against King Edwards. I came along and it seem like I was the missile that could get rid of Prince Buster... I made a whole heap of records with lyrics aimed at Prince Buster... 'Spit in the Sky', 'Joe Liges'... but Buster was like a super power, he stood his ground."   **Delroy Wilson**

On rare occasions Coxsone too would join in a session and he 'talked over' another of the early Delroy Wilson recordings aimed at Prince Buster.

"You could also say Coxsone was the first deejay 'cause on Delroy Wilson's 'King Pharaoh' it's him talking: 'When I say get down. I mean get down'."   **Bunny 'Striker' Lee**

Coxsone proved to be as adept and cool a business man as he was a sound system operator and in 1963 he opened his own studio and pressing plant: The Jamaican Recording and Publishing Studio. Better known as Studio One it was situated at 13 Brentford Road close to the Carib Theatre on the site of a former night club named The End. The original one track Ampex facilities were purchased from Federal when they upgraded to two tracks and Hedley Jones and Coxsone's cousin, Sid Bucknor, installed the facilities at Studio One and became its first engineers.

"And he went and bought this place down on Brentford Road, a club named The End, and his father built the studio there. His father was a master builder and he constructed the studio but he died later on. Coxsone's father and Sid Bucknor's mother were brother and sister so Coxsone and Sid was first cousins and Sidney was at Coxsone's studio for a little stint as an engineer... You have a guy named Hedley Jones. I don't know if he's still alive. And he put up most of those studios in Jamaica but the people don't talk about that... I think it was him who taught 'Sticky' Parks."

Bunny 'Striker' Lee

> **RADAR** the eyes and ears of radio won the war. The position might well have been reversed but for the efficient service done to Radar equipment with which allied planes were equipped. This same efficiency is now made available to you through **HEDLEY JONES' RADIO SERVICE.** 136 7/8 **KING ST.** where you will be able to obtain the services of a RADAR MECHANIC to do your radio service job. Phone 23422.

Hedley Jones had started selling records during the bop era in 1947 from his workshop and store called Bop City on King Street named after the legendary jazz club in New York. He imported records from England where he had served in the Royal Air Force.

"I got myself acquainted with the music scene in England so when I got back I knew exactly where to get my records. There was only one place in Jamaica where those records were obtainable at all and that was Bop City! I had been a radio engineer in the RAF and I got my training and built amplifiers that could differentiate between bass, treble and all that: tone controls, circuits and so forth. That was 1947 through 1952. All those years I was building these systems for people like Coxsone, who was known as Downbeat, for Duke Reid but one name that brought the sound to the top in Jamaica that has never been mentioned is 'Tom The Great Sebastian' for whom I built systems for. He started with a matinee show each Friday at a club called The Silver Slipper and at these shows new records started arriving: rhythm & blues.

I remained with it (Studio One) for one year doing recordings some of which have never seen the light of day.... These they called dubs and they just use them on the sound system for rivalry and they have never been in print at all. I did literally hundreds of these. I remember Saturday evenings in the studio for hours on end using an old primitive converted cutter to produce records for him."

Hedley Jones

Chapter 5

Jackie Mittoo in London UK 1985

The beginning of Jimmy Radway's journey along the long and difficult road to becoming a record producer began at this time. He was training to be an upholsterer and a friend of Jimmy's in the trade secured the contract to refurbish the club at the rear of 13 Brentford Road. Jimmy was introduced to Coxsone and "Mr Dodd was kind enough to let me sit in the studio while The Skatalites rehearsed. They were testing out the studio and I was always in the studio listening to what they were trying to do". He recalls sitting at the feet of Don Drummond while he played his trombone and this had a life changing effect on Jimmy. He consequently resolved to "push the upholstery and deal with the music" and started to write songs. He would eventually become one of the best, yet still underrated, producers of roots reggae music in the Seventies.

Like so many others Bob Marley & The Wailers began their careers at Studio One. Bob Marley was employed by Coxsone in 1963 as a talent scout and A&R man and one of his jobs was to play through stacks of imported records to find "a particular song for a singer" to cover. Bob actually lived at Brentford Road in a room "set up at the back" and it is said that Coxsone "acted as something of a surrogate father to Bob". Many of the most popular and influential Jamaican singers including Bob Andy, Horace Andy, Ken Boothe, Dennis Brown, Alton Ellis and Marcia Griffiths spent their formative years at Studio One but none were as highly regarded, or as well looked after, by Coxsone as the young Bob Marley.

The Skatalites, often credited on early Studio One releases as 'R Alphonso & Studio One Orchestra', provided the musical backbone for Coxsone's ska recordings. They broke up in the summer of 1965 and, the following year, as the music shifted towards rock steady Jackie Mittoo and Roland Alphonso went with Coxsone to Studio One to form the nucleus of Brentford Road's house band The Soul Brothers. Coxsone was justifiably proud of his musicians and featured photos of The Skatalites in session at Studio One on the cover of the 'Ska Authentic' album and dramatic action shots of the Soul Brothers on the 'Hot Shot' long player. The rapidly growing reputation of Studio One attracted Jamaica's talented singers and musicians like a magnet and Coxsone contracted many of them to work at Brentford Road.

Just what made the Studio One rhythm section so extra special has been a matter of much heated discussion and earnest debate over the years amongst musical scholars. Many of the musicians branched out on solo ventures but very few ever bettered the works that they made while at Brentford Road. The majority of the musicians also worked for other producers but they achieved an unmatched level of empathy and understanding at Studio One. Having an extremely talented band of musicians working at your own studio with no one watching the clock (studio time means money) gave considerable scope for experimentation and enabled everyone involved to push the boundaries still further. The backing tracks, or rhythms, that the house bands created at Studio One in the mid to late Sixties would become the foundation stone of reggae music.

"If I had my own studio I could spend more time for perfection… we had ten to twelve musicians employed weekly say Monday to Friday working from ten to five…I think we were the only person with a regular studio band playing weekly…" **Clement 'Coxsone' Dodd**

It is impossible to ever overstate Jackie Mittoo's role in the development of Studio One from this time onwards. He was pivotal to the success of the label and its place at the forefront of Jamaican musical history for Jackie was, in effect, the musical mastermind behind much of Coxsone's vast catalogue.

"But Jackie really turn out to be a musical giant as time go by…"
Clement 'Coxsone' Dodd

Donat Roy 'Jackie' Mittoo was beyond any doubt one of the most talented musicians and arrangers of his generation. Born in Browns Town, Jamaica 3rd March 1948 he grew up in York Castle, where his grandmother was a music teacher, and, from the age of three onwards, she taught him to play classical piano. He made his first public appearance at the age of ten. His first band, Jackie Mittoo's Ragtime Band, played rags and rhythm & blues and Jackie worked hard to reproduce on his piano the music that he had heard on the radio. His family moved to Kingston when Jackie was thirteen and he immediately joined The Rivals who were formed by Ansel Smart "a man who had money to buy an organ and a bass guitar but could not play either". The Rivals featured Tony Da Costa on lead vocals who had previously sang with Jimmy Haughton as The Deccas but they were not together for very long and Jackie left to join The Sheiks. Many members of The Sheiks would go on to greater things and the line up included Lloyd Knibb on drums, Lloyd Spence on bass, Lynn Taitt on guitar, Felix 'Deadly' Headley Bennett and Bobby Gaynair on saxophones, Roy Sterling (Lester's brother) and Johnny 'Dizzy' Moore on trumpets and Dobby Dobson, Keith 'Honey Boy Martin' Williams, Norma Frazer and Ken Lazarus on vocals. This stellar line up would entertain the audiences before the films started at cinemas such as The Majestic, The Tropical and The Rialto and they also played at clubs including The Sombrero and The Gunboat where they backed established local acts. The Sheiks eventually became known as The Cavaliers Orchestra.

By the time he entered High School Jackie was already a semi-professional musician alternating between playing piano for fun with his school friends at Kingston College in his lunch hour and playing seriously at the weekends in clubs and theatres with The Cavaliers. He was first approached by Coxsone when he was sitting in with Lynn Taitt and the house band at Federal Recording Studios.

"Jackie came to the attention of Recording Executive Clement S Dodd in Kingston Jamaica; and while still at school he worked as a staff musician for Coxsone Records appearing as a 'side man' on many recording dates for that label." **'Evening Time'**

When Coxsone opened his recording studio he asked Jackie to come and help him with the arrangement and development of songs. At first he was contracted to compose five new rhythms a week and, by the age of fifteen, Jackie had become the key figure in the Studio One set up as performer, arranger and talent scout. He also began to play piano and organ with The Skatalites. Jackie had been instrumental in the setting up of The Skatalites and, by the time ska had become a fully fledged musical form, Jackie's piano had become an integral part of its captivating rhythm. Coxsone updated Studio One to a pair of two track Ampex tape machines in 1965 as the music moved into an important new phase. The ska period proved to be relatively short lived but Jackie Mittoo was soon riding high on the crest of the next wave of musical invention to come out of Kingston. When the Skatalites broke up in 1965 Jackie formed The Soul Brothers who then became The Soul Vendors. Alongside Lynn Taitt's Jets, Tommy McCook's Supersonics, Jo Jo Bennett's Fugitives and Bobby Aitken's Carib Beats The Soul Vendors (occasionally, according to Derrick Morgan, featuring an uncredited Lynn Taitt 'moonlighting' on guitar) were responsible for establishing rock steady. His fellow ex-Skatalite, Tommy McCook, played a similar role for Coxsone's main musical rival throughout the Sixties and much of the cool magnificence of the Treasure Isle sound from Duke Reid down on Bond Street was directly attributable to the genius of Tommy McCook.

Paul Coote

In rock steady the organ became a regular addition to the rhythm section as the slower approach gave more space for it to be featured alongside the piano and guitar. Although it was still used mainly for intro lines and riffs in vocal tunes the organ began to play a more important role in the arrangements of backing tracks. Jackie would often play piano throughout a song and simultaneously play an organ fill with his right hand at appropriate moments. When The Heptones' debut record for Studio One, the risqué 'Fattie Fattie', was banned from Jamaican radio in 1967 Jackie created an instrumental version to the rhythm, or backing track, and played a moving soulful organ piece over it.

"They decided to ban it in Jamaica and, when they did that, everybody wanted to hear it so it made the record one of the best sellers in Jamaica."

Earl Morgan

Jackie named the record 'Ram Jam' in tribute to the celebrated club in Brixton, South London where The Soul Vendors had appeared on their UK tour in 1967 and it was a huge hit in both Jamaica and England.

"By the latter part of 1967 the Studio One label was important enough to warrant a tour of the UK headlined by two of its biggest stars. Singers Alton Ellis and Ken Boothe, with backing provided by a version of the Soul Vendors band, toured Jamaica during August as a warm up and then arrived in London in September for dates which would target England's black communities. Featured musicians included Jackie Mittoo, Roland Alphonso and trumpet player Johnny 'Dizzy' Moore and they were joined by veteran Jamaican singer Owen Gray who had emigrated to the UK some years earlier. Newspaper accounts have it that they played to packed houses, despite some reports that they were not so well attended, but the gig at Brixton's legendary 'Ram Jam' was such a success that Jackie Mittoo's organ cut to the Heptones' 'Fattie Fattie' was named after the club, adding to its notoriety."

Chris Lane

Count Suckle Cue Club
5a PRAED STREET, PADDINGTON, W.2
(under The Classic Cinema)

Proudly presents on Stage LIVE

The Return Performance of the

JAMAICA SOUL VENDORS
SATURDAY 28th OCTOBER

Featuring

ROLAND ALPHONSO, Tenor Sax
JOHNNY MOORE, Trumpet
JACKIE MITTON, Organ

Leading Singers

KEN BOOTHE, Latest Hit Record "PUPPET ON A STRING"
ALTON ELLIS, Latest Hit Record "GIRL, I HAD A DATE"

Come one, come all and see this **Big Last Performance** of this **Big Show** at the Cue Club.

also COUNT SUCKLE Sound System
Latest Soul Records from U.S.A. and Ja.

★ LADIES FREE NIGHTS THIS YEAR EVERY MONDAY & WEDNESDAY ★

Club opens seven nights a week. Sunday 7 p.m. - 5 a.m.
Monday to Thursday 5.30 p.m. - 4 a.m.   Licensed Bar

also Restaurant Open the whole night ★This Club is for members only.
Members of this Club must be at least 18 years of age.

Please apply for membership from COUNT SUCKLE
5a PRAED STREET, PADDINGTON. W.2   or   Telephone PAD 5274
Nearest Stations Paddington, Edgware Road   Buses 7 15

The Bell Press 286 Portobello Road W 10 LAD 0881

"These are the men that have set audiences Grooving All Night up and down the country at clubs like 'The Cue Club', Ram Jam', 'The 32 Club', 'The Roaring Twenties' and a host of other night spots and dancehalls." **'Soul Vendors On Tour'**

"It was still worth it though because it was the first time that people in this country had ever seen a real Jamaican band. There were artists like Lloyd Brevett, Alton Ellis, Roland Alphonso, Ken Boothe and Jackie Mittoo in that group… it was the first time that proper Jamaican music was played over here." **Junior Lincoln**

As rock steady developed into reggae the organ began to find its place in the rhythm section as Jackie, along with other acknowledged keyboard maestros such as Winston Wright, developed a style of playing that helped to drive the beat further forward. The organ became an important lead instrument and organ instrumentals, often with the addition of a film themed introduction or with an early deejay workout fashioned by playing over existing rhythm tracks, often proved to be more popular with record buyers than the original vocal versions. Jackie's career as a solo musician began to take shape with a series of solo albums for Studio One that exemplified all that the Hammond organ was capable of. He was able to wrest great depths of feeling from his chosen instrument and Jackie's name would become inextricably linked with the sound of the Hammond organ.

Jackie worked very closely with The Heptones' lead singer Leroy Sibbles whom he had taught to play bass. Coxsone ran regular Sunday auditions at Studio One and The Heptones (Leroy Sibbles, Barry Llewellyn & Earl Morgan) had travelled down to Brentford Road one Sunday afternoon in late 1966 where they auditioned in front of Bob Andy, Ken Boothe and Horace 'BB' Seaton of The Gaylads who was in charge of Studio One's A&R department at that time.

"Yes. I auditioned and passed several guys like Lloyd Parks as The Termites, The Heptones, The Melodians…" **Horace 'BB' Seaton**

The trio managed to pass this terrifying test and remained with Coxsone for the next five years and, despite 'Fattie Fattie' having been deemed too lewd for radio play, they soon became a vital part of the Studio One set up. Leroy Sibbles was employed as both talent scout and session bass player and Barry Llewellyn as a session musician. The countless bass lines created by Leroy Sibbles at Studio One were sufficiently melodic and versatile to take any amount of different arrangements or versions and have gone on to become an integral part of Jamaica's musical vocabulary. The Heptones also sang harmonies on other artists' tracks and their contribution to the sound of classic Studio One music is immense. They eventually left Studio One in 1971. Leroy Sibbles, in particular, was vociferous in his condemnation of how badly he felt The Heptones had been treated during their time at Brentford Road but Earl Morgan's attitude was more measured.

"I think if we had stayed with Coxsone we may have eventually gone on to become internationally famous but… it's one of them things."

Earl Morgan

Many artists described their time at Studio One as either being like going to college or as being part of a family. Things do not always run smoothly in a family situation and, like all families, there were disagreements but Horace Andy and Marcia Griffiths, for example, have always talked about their sojourn with Coxsone in unfailingly positive terms.

"I had to learn harmony, everything. That's why I love Studio One… That's where I learned to sing and sing harmony so I have no regrets."

Horace Andy

"It was really good… all the best people were at Studio One: Alton Ellis, Leroy Sibbles and Earl Morgan from The Heptones, Earl 'Bagga' Walker on bass… and I got to play all the instruments. They taught me at Studio One. That's where I learned everything. I always call it Studio First!"

Horace Andy

"Because any great singer you can think of that came out of Jamaica they all pass through Studio One. That's where you graduate…"

Marcia Griffiths

And if the artists were not playing, singing or singing harmonies then alternative employment could always be found."I used to help him (Coxsone) out with harmony singing. I was based there…"

Dennis Brown

"If you were up at Coxsone you had to play something, you had to sing something, do some harmonies or press some records."

Horace 'BB' Seaton

Working alongside Barry and Earl from The Heptones in the Studio One pressing plant was singer and deejay Dave Barker.

"I was beginning to make a family for myself. Dodd gave me the job."
Dave Barker

"Leroy played bass and Barry was in the studio playing organ and percussion. Most of the time I was in the factory… when I wasn't in the factory he had me singing harmonies…. Coxsone had said to me 'You look like a man who can deal with the record pressing part of the business'. So when I wasn't in the factory he had me singing harmonies."
Earl Morgan

The studio was also made available to other producers on Sundays when younger men, including Harry 'Moodisc' Mudie, Harry 'Harry J' Johnson and Bunny 'Striker' Lee cut hit records there. Errol 'ET'/'Errol T' Thompson worked at Brentford Road for a short while in 1969 and Max Romeo's infamous 'Wet Dream' for Bunny 'Striker' Lee was his first session as apprentice engineer.

"'Wet Dream' was a tune now! I put it on the 'Hold You Jack' rhythm and we voiced it up at Coxsone's studio. Max Romeo was a salesman. He was a good singer. He used to sing with his group called The Emotions but at that time he wasn't singing… it was Derrick Morgan's rhythm and he'd sung a different tune 'pon the rhythm and I said to Derrick: 'I want you to sing 'Wet Dream' but Derrick said 'No'. Coxsone had gone to the bathroom so I said to ET 'You take the tune' and Maxie started (sings) 'Every night me go to sleep me have wet dream…' and Coxsone came back and raised Cain! He said 'I don't want that tune recorded here!' and we had to stop the session because he wouldn't go no further. Anyway we got the tune mixed and sent it up to England to Mr Palmer. It was like a tune to make up the numbers. Next thing Mr. Palmer said to me that me and Maxie Romeo have to come to England…" **Bunny 'Striker' Lee**

'Wet Dream' spent twenty five weeks in the UK National Charts where it was released on Pama's Unity label. The BBC banned the record and disc jockey Alan Freeman would not mention its name on Sunday afternoon's chart run down on Radio One describing it as 'a record by Max Romeo'. Errol Thompson soon moved on to Randy's Studio 17 on North Parade.

But more often than not Coxsone would be on the road attending to business when the recordings were being made. And business was booming. By the close of the decade, in addition to the "ten to twelve" studio musicians and engineers and/or arrangers, Coxsone also employed "about fifty persons": twelve in the pressing plant (often artists and musicians), three shops employing two people at each of the premises, "four or five in the office" and three sales representatives. Coxsone also obtained the licence from Motown to press their records in Jamaica and adapted Berry Gordy's 'The Sound of Young America' slogan to 'The Sound of Young Jamaica' for his seven inch sleeve design and sponsored radio show.

"By the end of the Sixties Studio One was employing forty five people in the studio premises, by now also including a print shop for album sleeves and record presses which the producer had also acquired. There were five presses: four of these were used to manufacture up to four thousand seven inch vinyl 45 rpm singles during an eight hour shift. The fifth press was used for twelve inch vinyl which turned out around five hundred long playing albums in the same time." **Steve Barrow**

"Jackie Mittoo did all the arrangements for our stuff for Coxsone. Coxsone didn't actually produce the records. It was Jackie Mittoo arranging and engineers like Sid Bucknor and Sylvan Morris producing the session. Coxsone had the money and the studio." **Earl Morgan**

Jackie Mittoo then moved to Canada and, after settling in Toronto, he continued to regularly return to Jamaica and work at Studio One, but the label lost a large degree of focus and direction when Jackie was no longer at Brentford Road on a full time basis. While in Canada Jackie played with visiting Jamaican artists, set up his own Stine Jac label and actually became very well known there as a purveyor of 'easy listening' music through his work for the Canadian Talent Library.

Highly respected throughout the reggae world as an elder statesman who was always willing to share his knowledge Jackie Mittoo's untimely death from cancer on 16th December 1990 in Toronto, Canada robbed reggae music of one its most inspirational figures. He helped to build, refine and define reggae as we now understand it and his work, and its far reaching influence, deserves far wider recognition. It would not be enough to simply describe Jackie Mittoo as one of the greatest keyboard players to ever come out of Jamaica although he undoubtedly was. It is his towering influence on the development of reggae as a composer and arranger that is truly remarkable and his absolute authority over a genre that, probably more than any other single figure, he helped to create.

"Jackie has done so much for Jamaican music. Jackie is a supreme voice in this business. Jackie came to the studio as a young boy going to school... he would come to the studio from school three o'clock every evening and get involved. And one day Jackie came like eleven o'clock like all of us in his ordinary clothes not his school uniform. Then we know that school was over for Jackie. Jackie finished with school...

Everything that was played was from Jackie's mind because he was telling the bass man what to play, he was telling the guitarist what to play, the horns and he was directing the whole studio while playing with one hand. Only Jackie knew when to come in. So he would play and count us in at the same time and direct us in." **Alton Ellis**

Fitzroy 'Larry' Marshall also played an important, if still unrecognised, role at Brentford Road. Born 17th December 1941 at Lawrence Park in the parish of St Ann he came to Kingston in 1957 and his first solo recordings were released on Justin 'Philip' Yap's Top Deck and Tuneico labels. He came to prominence towards the end of the sixties alongside Alvin Leslie as one of the duo Larry & Alvin and their first recording for Coxsone in 1968, 'Nanny Goat', heralded the arrival of the faster reggae beat and was followed by further hits including 'Hush Up', 'Mean Girl' and 'Throw Me Corn'. Larry Marshall went on to not only sing lead and harmonies on reggae and gospel recordings at Studio One but also run auditions and help to write, arrange and produce records for Horace Andy, Dennis Brown, Burning Spear and Freddie McKay. His ability to pick hits was unerring but, even if you did manage to get your song recorded at Studio One, there was no guarantee it would ever be released on record.
"Because actually I still have at least sixty percent of my stuff unreleased. You understand?" **Clement 'Coxsone' Dodd**

"In fact Coxsone had long had a policy of making music with just about anyone who walked through the door and his catalogue is testament to that. For all the big hits, and retrospective hits, and the classic, much loved and licked-over rhythms that have emerged from Studio One, there are scores of lesser known, but still top quality, tunes that fell through the cracks at the original time of release but have been recognised, eventually, as the true musical gems that they are.

Many of the tunes produced at Studio One were 'uncommercial' to say the least, and it's hard to imagine that someone with the business sense and experience of Clement Dodd would ever imagine that they would sell enough to recoup the recording costs, so it's all the more miraculous that so much of this music was committed to tape…" **Chris Lane**

The Royals had changed their name to The Tempests after The Temptations in 1967 as "our singing was closer to the US sound but the Jamaican producers were not ready. If it wasn't gimmicks you never stand a chance". Lee Perry had turned them down at their first Brentford Road audition and, on their second audition, BB Seaton also turned them down but it proved to be third time lucky. Coxsone himself was in charge of their third audition and this time the group passed the test. In spring 1969 The Royals recorded eight songs at Studio One, including the first version of their classic 'Pick Up The Pieces', none of which were released at the time. The Royals recorded their own version of 'Pick Up The Pieces' for their Uhuru label which became a huge hit in 1973 and, after Larry Marshall had found the tape, the Studio One version to 'Pick Up The Pieces' was released. It was initially credited to The Tempests but on later pressings the name was changed to The Royals

"It was Lee Perry used to do the auditioning for Coxsone… him turned me down. I had to go back again! 'Cause them days when you get turned down you can't show your face the next week, you know, you have to go back all three month's time, six month's time 'cause the man tell you go home and practise then come back. 'Cause them days it was one take and if you a sing something brilliant (sings) yeah, yeah ooohhh… and then you made a mistake the engineer would say 'come from the top again'. Hundreds of men recorded and the producer never put it out. Coxsone never wanted to put out 'Pick Up The Pieces' and if it wasn't for Larry Marshall it would never have seen the light of day. The first Studio One pressing was credited to The Tempests but I would never record a song and then record it over. I would have left it if I'd known it was going to come out because if I did sing something for a producer I'd never sing it back. We

asked Coxsone if he could change the name and he allowed it. It was the only thing he ever gave us." **Roy Cousins**

Also on the same tape were 'Where It's At' by Lloyd Forest and 'Live Up To Your Name' by Prince Lincoln and these two tunes, now also rightly regarded as Studio One classics, were also given a belated release.

"I went to Studio One... there was no auditioning thing! Coxsone wasn't there. Morris, great guy, and Larry Marshall and Enid from Keith and Enid as well. I just went there and go into the studio and said I'd like to go on some rhythms. Just like that! I told Sylvan Morris... Larry Marshall was actually working in the studio at the time and Enid... they were all working in Coxsone's studio. They were the ones who'd find the tapes them. The first song we did was 'Nanny Version' (a version to Larry & Alvin's 'Nanny Goat') and from him hear that he said he wanted an LP and that was it. And when I was working for Coxsone Duke Reid called me... no it wasn't Duke it was the engineer Byron Smith." **Dennis AlCapone**

Larry was also assistant engineer to Sylvan Morris for three and a half years but he later stated that he always felt Sylvan Morris was holding back on teaching him and in 1974 he left Studio One to work with Carlton Patterson's Black & White label. But even after they had left Studio One Mr Dodd's ex-employees would continue to recommend other artists to work at Brentford Road as Winston Rodney, The Burning Spear, recalled:

"Both of us are from the parish of St Ann. I bumped into Bob (Marley) and I asked him who and where I could check. He told me about Studio One. We have a nice reasoning pertaining to the recording business. But start with Clement Dodd. You ain't going to stay with Clement Dodd forever." **Winston 'Burning Spear' Rodney**

The international success of Bob Marley & The Wailers in 1975 brought about an increased interest in what was now being termed roots music and, when people began to investigate the roots, they discovered that not only was Coxsone the first to record Winston Rodney, The Burning Spear, but that his catalogue also delved far deeper into this genre than had previously been imagined. Burning Spear's sombre 1969 Supreme release of 'Door Peeper'/'Door Peep Shall Not Enter' along with The Abyssinians' hymn like 'Satta Amasa Gana' proved to be the harbingers of all that followed. The Abyssinians' record was a self production released on their own Clinch label that same year but its timeless rhythm had been provided by The Sound Dimension down on Brentford Road with Leroy Sibbles originating the immortal bass line. The record owed a musical debt to Neal Hefti's 'The Mafista' from the 1966 'Batman' soundtrack and took some of its lyrical inspiration from Carlton & His Shoes' 'Happy Land' 1968 release on Supreme, however, it demonstrated how these widely disparate influences could be diverted and directed into making something totally original and intensely moving. 'Declaration Of Rights', also from The Abyssinians, was a Coxsone production and was almost as brilliant. Records like these, pleas for self-determination full of brooding introspection or devotional joy, were inspirational to the new wave of artists and producers. Their subsequent appropriation of the Studio One catalogue would ensure the legendary status of Coxsone's pioneering work.

"The first time I heard Coxsone do one tune I laughed. I said 'You're mad man! Where are you going to sell that?' A tune called 'Sounds From The Burning Spear' ('Door Peeper'/'Door Peep Shall Not Enter'). When Burning Spear came out they probably didn't sell in the shops but the sound men liked it because these tunes have some fantastic bass lines. Like the 'Joe Frazier' rhythm. I told Coxsone 'Jackson you have tune on tape name 'Joe Frazier'? It mash up the place.' He didn't know the tune until I started humming it then he said 'Oh! You mean 'He Prayed'?' I said 'Yes. Burning Spear'. The first album he did with Burning Spear ('Studio One Presents Burning Spear') I said 'Boy you're brave!' And then Burning Spear started coming with the hits. He put it out and everyone started doing over these rhythms. That kind of chanting thing was different to the kind of singing I used to deal with but afterwards you had to adjust everything because you don't know which one will hit. Once upon a time a man like Pat Kelly hit with the Curtis Mayfield thing then everybody wanted Pat Kelly or Slim Smith or Dave Barker who had sweet voices and then they were the hardest voices to sell. Yes. Because the rough voice, the rough 'rockstone' voice, now they were the voice." **Bunny 'Striker' Lee**

Coxsone was one of the first producers to actively encourage and record Rastafarian inspired music and the music that Burning Spear made at Studio One between 1969 and 1974 was totally at odds with much of the music of the time. The formats and themes that they explored together did not begin to encroach on reggae music until later in the decade when their influence would become all encompassing.

"We worked with various musicians, not one set all the time. Leroy 'Horse Mouth' Wallace used to be the drummer there. Leroy Sibbles played a lot of bass in the day. Jackie Mittoo and Ernest Ranglin were there also. Some greats! It was more like a college." **Winston 'Burning Spear' Rodney**

"Him was a good disciplinarian... a lot of the man there with him at that time never had no father like myself and, trust me, he was good father figure even though he wasn't giving nothing away! But Coxsone gave you something that the other producers didn't. He gave you respect. The other producers aren't giving you nothing and treat you with contempt... treat you like a piece of sh*t. Coxsone didn't. Anywhere you see him he'd say 'Hello Jackson'... you know he called everybody Jackson. You understand me? That's how he was but you know your place with Coxsone... you don't cross that line." **Roy Cousins**

Albums were not a regular feature of a music driven by seven inch singles but, unlike the majority of his contemporaries, and completely against prevailing trends, Coxsone had persevered with recording numerous albums throughout the Sixties and the Seventies where his artists were allowed to explore different avenues away from the restrictions of a seven inch hit single. These albums were not hurriedly thrown together to capitalise on a hit single but were thoughtful, considered reflective compendiums such as Horace Andy's 'Skylarking', Burning Spear's 'Studio One Presents' and 'Rocking Time', Alton Ellis' 'Sings Rock And Soul' and 'Sunday Coming', The Heptones' with 'The Heptones' and 'On Top', Roland Alphonso's 'King Of Sax' and Jackie Mittoo's 'Evening Time' and 'Macka Fat'. These, and numerous other long playing Studio One sets, represent the pinnacle of many Jamaican vocalists' and musicians' artistic achievements.

In the early Seventies a new generation of artists and record producers came to the fore who had grown up surrounded by the sound of Studio One and who possessed a very real sense of both its history and its importance. The Studio One name was so well established that many were unaware of where many Brentford Road 'originals' had originated. 'Darker Shade Of Black', credited to The Soul Vendors on the Studio One label in 1968, was a very popular instrumental cut to The Beatles' 'Norwegian Wood (This Bird Has Flown)' from their 1965 'Rubber Soul' album. In 1974 Leonard 'Santic' Chin versioned the tune in the prevailing rockers style as 'Harder Shade Of Black' with Richard 'Dirty Harry' Hall playing tenor saxophone backed with 'Better Shade Of Dub' which led to a showdown with Coxsone over 'his' tune!

"After 'Harder Shade Of Black' Mr Dodd come look for me! He wanted to thump me in the head because I'd done over his tune so I had to hold off out of Randy's for a few days! I didn't know it was a Beatles tune then because his name was on the label as the writer! It was Leroy Sibbles played the bass on it (Leroy had played bass on the Soul Vendors cut) and 'Tin Leg' (Lloyd Adams) on drums. But after all that when I saw Mr Dodd… I think he was surprised to see me being so young… he was alright. To me he was an old man! So Mr Dodd said 'that youth doesn't look like the rest of them rude boys! So just 'low him'." **Leonard 'Santic' Chin**

And these younger producers and musicians, many of whom had learnt their craft at Brentford Road, began to make their mark with the new 'rebel rock' sound.

"'Real Rock', 'Swing Easy'… me did love them tune! It's music me a talking. Me listen to anything named 'instrumental'. The Skatalites with Jackie Mittoo… them me really love!" **Augustus Pablo**

Throughout the decade Bunny 'Striker' Lee, the Hookim brothers at Channel One, Augustus Pablo, The Mighty Two (Joe Gibbs & Errol T) and many, many more began to use Jamaica's musical past as the primary source of inspiration for their current work. In doing so they fashioned the future of reggae music as they cut hit record after hit record after hit record with updates of Studio One rhythms. Many of their versions became better known than the original cuts which occasionally led to long and protracted court battles over the ownership of the original songs especially when they formed the basis for a 'crossover' international hit record. The origins of Musical Youth's 'Pass the Dutchie' lay, via The Mighty Diamonds 'Pass The Kutchie', in The Sound Dimension's 'Full Up'. Althea & Donna's 'Up Town Top Ranking' came, via Trinity's 'Three Piece Suit', from Alton Ellis' 'I'm Still In Love'. Both 'Full Up' and 'I'm Still In Love' were originally recorded at Studio One. The root of the problem was in the fact that, at the time, very few had ever considered the long term implications of the way the music was composed, performed, recorded and credited. This now had to be worked out in the courtroom which invariably meant that the lawyers, as always, were the ones who made the most money.

The reliance of much of the reggae business on Studio One rhythms in the Seventies and Eighties has meant that the Studio One dub albums are of particular interest. When it comes down to it dub is only as good as the original rhythm track is and, if a Studio One rhythm is being worked on, then it is difficult to go too far wrong. Coxsone was one of the first producers to realise the importance of releasing dub albums and he eventually issued many more than his contemporaries which is unsurprising when one considers the number of rhythms that originated at Studio One. The first, and reckoned to be the best, of the Studio One dub long players were 'Hi Fashion Dub' and 'Dub Store Special'. These albums might sound relatively unsophisticated compared to the standards set by dub masters such as King Tubby and Errol 'Errol T' Thompson but Coxsone, who did all the mixing, was working on two track tapes and had to rely solely on his innate sense of timing.

"Studio One Dub Classics are exclusive combinations of sound track originals brilliantly coloured and dramatic in details. There's a great selection of real JUK'S and DUB in this album. From the mellow 60's to the bold 'Disco Sound' of today still glitters. They'll light up your life.

Special Thanks: Jackie Mittoo, Richard Ace, Earl 'Bagga' Walker, Cedric Brooks, Dennis Campbell, Leroy Sibbles, Eric Frater, Leroy 'Horsey' Wallace, Freddie McGregor and all other musicians who have contributed in making this album possible."
'Juk's Incorporation Parts One & Two'

"The bass lines in particular laid the foundation for all the Jamaican music that was to follow, with players such as Bryan Atkinson, Boris Gardiner and Leroy Sibbles remaining largely uncredited for their illustrious efforts despite the significance of their work." **Chris Lane**

For the first time music lovers were able to appreciate the work, stripped back to its basic components, of the many different Brentford Road musical aggregations and the overwhelming contribution of the engineering skills of Sylvan Morris. "When Coxsone first started out he had a whole heap of disappointment but when Sylvan Morris left WIRL and went with him as an engineer... Coxsone developed a sound for himself." **Bunny 'Striker' Lee**

"Sylvan Morris ran the studio sessions. In fact, Morris really created the trademark 'sound' of Studio One and advised artists how to get the best results from their sessions although Coxsone himself decided which tracks would be released; he would also make suggestions about which 'foreign' songs would be recorded." **Steve Barrow**

Sylvan Morris was born in 1949 and studied at Jamaica Technical High School on Hanover Street and started work at WIRL in 1965 where he assisted chief engineer, Graeme Goodall, on the three track recorder. Sylvan learnt the art of engineering from Graeme Goodall and would later credit him as "his mentor". He then moved to Duke Reid's Treasure Isle for six months before replacing Sid Bucknor as the chief engineer at Studio One in 1968 at the age of nineteen. Morris considers this to be "the turning point" in his career and he would stay at Brentford Road for six years. It was not long before he took on much more than the role of engineer.

"I would say he (Coxsone) did a certain amount of mixing but when I went there the bulk of the work came to me... to be truthful I would say I was both the engineer, the producer and arranger." **Sylvan Morris**

"Duke knew what he wanted. Coxsone knew too but Coxsone used to leave the musicians like Jackie Mittoo and them guys to do the things for him. Sylvan Morris was a great engineer... he used to be at WIRL before he went to Coxsone. Morris used to tell the musicians what he wanted and when Coxsone came in the evening after a hard day's work cutting stampers and things he'd listen and say 'Morris... mix these four or five tunes and I'll cut them tomorrow'. So Coxsone had good hearing." **Bunny 'Striker' Lee**

As Roy Cousins rightfully pointed out if the first take was not up to standard then even the best mixing engineer in the business could get very little out of it and, when it came to the first take, Sylvan Morris was rated as Kingston's foremost recording engineer. "He's the greatest. Any artist will tell you that. He's so good that if it wasn't for him Studio One wouldn't exist. He's a qualified electronics technician and before he went to Studio One the board would break down every five minutes but he did repair it. From Sylvan Morris went to Studio One there were no problems. Coxsone's best mic.? It's Sylvan Morris make it! Any time he did a recording he took out the valves and cooled them. Jamaica is not a cold country and in later years studios started to put in air conditioning but before they'd tell you to wait outside for an hour or two and then you could come back in. He's the backbone of Studio One and no-one gives him no credit! Same thing at Harry J's.

No-one ever complained about Sylvan Morris... but he never get the credit."
Roy Cousins

"Sylvan Morris was full of vibes. When you're recording with an engineer like Sylvan Morris him give you good vibes you know. He's always dancing... you know what I mean? Anytime you see him stop dancing you know something's wrong. That's what I love about him. Out of all the engineers Morris was my engineer."
Dennis AlCapone

And, as Sylvan Morris recalled, the best results were not necessarily about having the most expensive equipment:

"… but Ampex is a very good machine, the tape recorder itself, but the actual console was a Lang. It wasn't the top of the line. He had some good equalisers, Pultec equaliser and so forth but what I'm saying is that the sound came from the actual knowledge of myself and the musicians."
Sylvan Morris

Sylvan Morris' role at Studio One, his technical ability and his musical understanding proved to be a winning combination and he established methods of working and ways of using equipment that were every bit as important to the overall Studio One sound as the contributions of the musicians.

"You're coming from town
Your face turned to this sound
On your way up
Or on your way down
I want you to stop at this station for identification
I'm going to turn you over to your Sound Dimension
Your music producer… everybody on the ball!"
'More Scorchia' Sound Dimension

The name of one of Studio One's seminal session bands was actually taken from an echo and reverb unit, purchased in London for sixty guineas (a guinea was one pound and one shilling or £1.05 pence) during the Soul Vendors' 1967 tour. Soundimension was a freestanding echo unit created by Ivor Arbiter, a British technician "a compact portable device providing echo and reverberation effects when used in conjunction with any audio amplifying system" which was vital to the creation of the classic Studio One sound.

Clement 'Coxsone' Dodd
Coxsone's Music City 3135 Fulton Street Brooklyn New York USA 19th August 1992

"…These chaps used to have a name that they gave me. They call me 'My Engineer'. Now the reason for that was at the time I was very strong in getting the tune to sound a particular way in which I liked. So when they would formulate a rhythm we tried to get it to sound a particular way… if you are familiar with a lot of the rhythms you will hear Soundimension piece of equipment that he brought there." **Sylvan Morris**

"Morris was the one in charge of the studio… 100% in my time… but if you look 'pon the Studio One sleeves Morris no get no credit 'pon them. You understand me? And if Morris didn't go to Studio One maybe it wouldn't be so big till this day. I remember one time Morris closed the studio down for a week and repaired everything so Coxsone automatically had an engineer and a repair man. And in Jamaica they will tell you the man who we call engineer is the man like Morris who can repair the board but the rest of the men, who can't repair the board, we call them operator. Don't forget that!" **Roy Cousins**

"And you have to talk about the engineer Sylvan Morris…a great engineer as he was an electronics expert too… who was at Coxsone studio. Plenty of people don't talk about that engineer but you would a call him 'Studio One' because him used to have the sound. He put the guitars through the phaser (Soundimension). Only Coxsone alone have that sound… a kind of repeating sound 'keh keh keh'. We used to call them 'Frater'… the 'Frater' was Eric Frater the guitarist. 'Cause if Frater play it without it at a different studio it never worked. 'Cause Harry Mudie's 'Drifter' with Dennis Walks was built at Coxsone's studio and Frater alone had that sound… You understand? But Sylvan Morris was the backbone of Studio One. Coxsone used to do some engineering too but Sylvan Morris… we used to like that sound but we didn't have the Soundimension thing that Coxsone brought from England. That Studio One sound that developed… like it's Morris. Morris was an engineer and a technician in one. You understand? He taught Errol Thompson too…

What I used to rate Coxsone for was they'd go right through the day and make some tunes and when Coxsone used to come in the evening after he came off the road, him and a guy named Bim Bim ('Coxsone's right hand man'), used to be out cutting stampers and delivering records. And he'd come in the evening and he'd get a quart of white rum and him build him spliff and he'd start smoking his spliff and drinking his white rum and he'd say 'Morris. Make I hear what you a do today' and Morris start play

it and he'd say: 'Mix this. Mix that' and his selection was right! When he first put out Burning Spear I said 'Where you a go with that? You're a mad man!' but he'd say 'Yes Jack!' and when come and you look 'pon the Burning Spear today… so he was a great selector. But when it came to producing… most of Coxsone's tunes it's the musicians that make them like Jackie Mittoo and Denzil Laing 'cause Coxsone was out on the road."
Bunny 'Striker' Lee

"Most producers sit and watch but that is not a true producer. It used to be like that at Studio One. Jackie Mittoo would do the work and Coxsone would not be present. They are good A&R people though! For example if a singer like Horace Andy came to me I probably would not have recorded him. Coxsone saw something in that voice and it worked."
Cleveland 'Clevie' Browne

Sylvan Morris left Studio One in 1974 and, following his departure, the bulk of the engineering work was handled by Coxsone. As the Seventies progressed Jamaica's musical history provided a seemingly endless source of inspiration and the importance of the Studio One rhythm section became increasingly apparent.

"…practically all of Coxsone's tunes have been done over by other producers. They sort of use them as a pattern, so it's a standard as such you know."
Sylvan Morris

The late Seventies and early Eighties trend for updating old rhythms and adding new songs was not new but what was different this time was the way in which it soon took over the entire reggae business. Unfortunately, while some did this brilliantly, many more missed the point completely. Lincoln 'Sugar' Minott's 1978 debut long playing release, 'Live Loving' for Studio One, showed all that could be done when a singer and songwriter as talented as Sugar was allowed to work with a selection of original Studio One rhythms. Sugar had convinced Coxsone to record him after arriving at his audition with a song that fitted an existing rhythm track and felt that Mr Dodd was interested because "he don't have to go and make no music". He signed a contract for one year but would stay at Studio One for six years. His impact was profound and 'Vanity', his adaptation of Alton Ellis' 'I'm Just A Guy', would soon become better known than Alton's original hit. Sugar continued to demonstrate his mastery of writing songs that sounded as if they'd been written expressly for an existing rhythm track and would go on to become one of the key figures in reggae music through his own productions for his Black Roots and Youth Promotion labels. Coxsone's recycling ethic extended to using a job lot of Winro and Forward labels and 'look/listen & learn Audio Visual Edukit' twelve inch sleeves that he had purchased in America. The sleeves were often used as they came but a number were overprinted with titles and track listings for Studio One dub albums including 'Ital Dub' and 'Better Dub'.

After starting work with King Tubby in 1977 Overton 'Scientist' Browne did a brief stint at Studio One in 1979 to learn live recording. His first session was with Peter Broggs and he went on to record overdubs with Pablove Black, Earl 'Bagga' Walker and then drum overdubs with Freddie McGregor. His early mixes coincided with Studio One's first forays into the 'dance hall style'. Sugar Minott's 'Oh Mr DC', where The Tennors' 'Pressure & Slide' was updated into a marijuana anthem, is usually credited as one of the first Scientist mixes but, after conflicting ideas with Mr Dodd about how to record, Scientist returned to King Tubby's Dromilly Avenue studio.

At the turn of the decade two further albums, "produced by, arranged by and all engineering by CS Dodd", largely made up of new songs gently crafted on to old but subtly remixed Brentford Road rhythms, revitalised Studio One. Johnny Osbourne's 'Truth & Rights' and Freddie McGregor's 'Bobby Bobylon' albums led the way where others could only follow. The deejay duo Papa Michigan & General Smiley brought a whole new lease of life to 'Real Rock' when they interpreted the rhythm as 'Nice Up The Dance' and 'Love Bump', The Lone Ranger's adaptation of Slim Smith's 'Rougher Yet', sold out every time it re-appeared in the shops.

"I actually worked at Studio One for several years from about 1978. It was like a school to me. I had a chance to listen to tracks directly from the master tapes. I did overdubs on many of the old Studio One rhythms, some of The Skatalites stuff, we added like percussion stuff on it."
Cleveland 'Clevie' Browne

These classic releases introduced a way of working that sadly, in the hands of lesser talents, would lead the music into a cul de sac that Wayne Smith's 'Under Me Sleng Teng' eventually showed a way out of in 1984. When the dance hall style worked there was very little to better it but, for the first time ever, when critics again decided that reggae "all sounds the same" there really was no answer. It was difficult to see, for example, how many more versions of Slim Smith's sublime '(I'll) Never Let Go', now known as 'The

Answer' after The Lone Ranger's 1977 hit deejay version, the record buying public would be able to take especially when the majority were on rhythms that were less than strong do-overs of the original Brentford Road versions.

"By 1983, indeed, it was unusual for anyone to have a Jamaican hit employing a completely original rhythm track."
Steve Barrow & Peter Dalton

Looking back is one thing but not moving forward is another thing entirely. It was obvious that the public were completely bemused and confused when younger customers came into record shops asking if "Slim Smith had any new records out this week" when Slim Smith had been dead for over ten years. But records by Slim Smith, such as the aforementioned '(I'll) Never Let Go' and 'Rougher Yet', were selling far more than new records due to the popularity and preponderance of their dance hall versions. It worked for a while, and could probably work again, but the dance hall style was rapidly reduced to a formula consisting of lyrics carelessly sung or deejayed about "rub a dubbing in the dance" over a substandard recut of one of about ten Studio One rhythms. However, this was hardly the fault of anyone down on Brentford Road.

The 'Top One Hundred Rhythms 1984 to 1985' sampled from one thousand LP's and published in Small Axe fanzine in 1988 might give some indication of just how much Jamaican music had come to rely on rhythm tracks from Brentford Road. All but two out of the Top Ten are Studio One productions and one of these, 'Satta Amassa Gana', was recorded at Studio One with The Sound Dimension.

1. Real Rock - The Sound Dimension – Studio One
2. Jah Shakey – Roland Alphonso – Studio One
3. Satta Amasa Gana – The Abyssinians – Clinch
4. Heavenless – Vincent 'Don D Junior' Gordon – Studio One
5. Never Let Go – Slim Smith – Studio One
6. Party Time – The Heptones – Studio One
7. Full Up - The Sound Dimension - Studio One
8. Shank I Sheck – Bobby Ellis & The Revolutionaries – High Note
9. Drum Song – Jackie Mittoo – Studio One
10. I'm Just A Guy – Alton Ellis – Studio One

When the first digital rhythms began to make their mark many of their origins could also be traced back to Studio One: Thriller's minimal but monstrous 'Tickle Me' for Sly & Robbie's Taxi label used the bass line from Keith McCarthy's rock steady rude boy anthem 'Every Body Rude Now'... so perhaps there was still "no new thing new under the sun".

The Studio One legend continued to grow. When Leroy George 'Peckings' Price opened his Studio One Record Shop at 142 Askew Road in Shepherds Bush, West London in the Autumn of 1975 he opened the eyes (and ears) of an entire generation of UK music lovers to the vast range and scope of the Studio One catalogue. Peckings enjoyed a close, lifelong relationship with Coxsone and had previously sold Studio One records from his house and advised Coxsone for years before he opened the shop.

"Coxsone used to cover the tunes and the tunes were hits up here... Peckings used to tell him 'do over this one... it a sell over here' and Coxsone would do it." **Bunny 'Striker' Lee**

"However, there is now a totally different kind of shop that has just opened at 142 Askew Road, Shepherds Bush, London W12 devoted almost entirely to selling Coxsone music." **Chris Lane**

The Askew Road store stocked the latest and the greatest of Brentford Road's staggering output together with an unbelievable array of oldies. A trip to the shop would invariably be heavy on the wallet, and a learning process too, for Peckings was always ready to share his knowledge and insight and would tell tales of the "good old days". Sadly he died of a heart attack in 1994. His sons continue with the same proud tradition to this day through their retail premises on Askew Road and their innovative productions and excellent compilation albums.

"Mr Peckings took great pleasure in providing a musical service to the public and was an inspiration to all music lovers."
'Studio One Presents Tribute To Peckings'

After armed robbers held up his Brentford Road headquarters in the early Eighties Coxsone relocated to the USA where, after a brief sojourn in Long Island, he opened Coxson's Music City, a shop and recording studio, at 3135 Fulton Street, Brooklyn, New York. The American manufactured records from this period are now highly sought after by collectors because of their superior pressing quality. While in New York he continued to re-release his classic back catalogue and record new artists including Earl Sixteen and the prolific Frankie Paul, and establsihed artists too, on old and new rhythms.

"Earl observed that all of the then top producers were 'licking back Studio One rhythms' so he began to visit Studio One on Brentford Road where he told Mr Dodd 'I want to do a tune for you but I want to sing on the original rhythms.' Mr Dodd felt that Earl 'wasn't ready to sing on a record' but Earl had decided to 'stay with Studio One' although he 'waited for months before I got a look in.' A good friend of Earl's, a music teacher at Norman Manley Secondary School, had written a song for him but 'the song had too much lyrics! I was singing, singing, singing and Mr Dodd gave me a box of records and told me to choose one and try and fit the song on it. I picked 'Fight It To The Top' by the Heptones (also known as 'Heptones Gonna Fight') and cut out most of the verses.'

The resulting song 'Love Is A Feeling' became an instant classic when released on a Studio One seven inch single and made such an impact that this ever popular rhythm is now often referred to as Earl Sixteen's very own 'Love Is A Feeling' rhythm. They did a total of eighteen songs together and Earl 'still hasn't finished!' although a superb selection, along with their attendant instrumental versions, were released in 1985 as the 'Earl Sixteen Show Case', now regarded as one of the essential items in Coxsone Dodd's extensive long playing catalogue. Earl was fulsome in his praise of Mr Dodd 'Him pay me good! Every time I see Sir D he have a money for me' and Coxsone presented Earl with 'three hundred dollars and a gold watch.' He was the only producer to ever tell Earl that his records were selling and he found this particularly heartening and encouraging."

Harry Hawke

The Brentford Road building, despite having been extensively and expensively upgraded to sixteen track recording, became a warehouse and storeroom with the legendary King Stitt left in charge to complete the wholesale orders. By the end of the decade the premises were beginning to look badly run down and the Studio One sign, blown down by Hurricane Gilbert in 1988, still remained smashed in pieces on the ground in the front yard three years later.

But later that year Coxsone celebrated thirty five years in the music business with two huge concerts in Kingston and Montego Bay named '1956 to 1991 The Beat Goes On' featuring a stellar line up of artists who had recorded for Studio One over the years. Many artists returned to Jamaica to perform and pay tribute to Coxsone and were sufficiently dignified to put any ill feelings from the past behind them. Others were unable to forget their rancour over alleged bad treatment and described the concerts as 'The Beating Goes On'. That same year Coxsone was awarded Jamaica's third highest honour, the Order Of Distinction, for his services to the country. Following his mother's death in 1998 he returned to Kingston where he refurbished and reopened the studio and began to make music once more at Brentford Road. In April 2004 the Jamaican government renamed Brentford Road 'Studio One Boulevard'.

Always working to reach a wider audience for his music Coxsone signed several international pressing and distribution deals over the years with varying degrees of success. Many early releases from Studio One were pressed in the UK on the Blue Beat, Ska Beat, R&B, Island, Blue Cat, and Doctor Bird labels. Towards the end of the Sixties Island/B&C gave Mr Dodd his own, regrettably short lived, London based labels, Coxsone and Studio One, run by North London entrepreneur Junior Lincoln who also released a handful of Coxsone's gospel productions on the Tabernacle label. The records released on these labels were usually clean pressings and are now highly prized, and consequently highly priced, among the collecting fraternity and, with UK catalogue numbers, you can complete the set. In 1969 Junior Lincoln started to release Studio One productions on the Bamboo and Banana labels from his shop, Junior's Music Spot, in Stroud Green Road, Finsbury Park, North London. Unfortunately, these records were frequently overshadowed by the releases on Trojan's and Pama's numerous labels which benefitted from better distribution networks. Junior Lincoln closed down the operation in 1972 to establish the Ashanti label and the following year "much of the liquidated stock was sold off to the public at 10p a time in the stores of the UK supermarket chain Tesco". These Bamboo and Banana releases were scorned for many years by the self appointed cognoscenti but have belatedly begun to fetch high prices on the collectors market.

In 1983 Coxsone signed with the Massachusetts, USA based Heartbeat Records who have done a superb job in packaging, annotating, promoting and distributing Studio One music worldwide always with the type of top quality presentation that it deserves. From the late Nineties onwards the London based Soul Jazz label have released an excellent selection of thoughtful, comprehensively compiled releases that have considerably raised the profile of Studio One outside of the traditional reggae audience. And, in the New Millennium, Dub Store Records in Japan have added to the canon with a superb selection of facsimile seven inch Studio One singles in the original 'Coxson's Dramatic & Music Centre' sleeves.

"Thank God for the effort I made when I was younger to dedicate myself to putting out the music. The music I've produced is timeless and the demand for it is simply limitless." **Clement 'Coxsone' Dodd**

Not long after completing work on an album with London based vocal group, The Blackstones, Clement Seymour 'Coxsone' Dodd died of a heart attack on 4th May 2004 aged 72. His wife and their children continued to license and release his enormous back catalogue but Norma Dodd died in September 2010 and the children now look after Studio One. The extent of Coxsone's legacy is immeasurable and it is indisputable that, more than any other studio or label, Studio One shaped and fashioned the sound of reggae music as it is now understood.

Peter 'Studio P' Roberts 3rd July 1954 to 16th September 2007
This chapter is respectfully dedicated, or livicated, to the memory of Peter Roberts: a good friend and the foremost collector of and acknowledged authority on Studio One. As Freddie McGregor succinctly stated: 'To Bro Peter: Give thanks for the preservation of the archives.'

The Jamaican Recording and Publishing Studio
13 Brentford Road, Kingston 5

Producer:
Clement 'Coxsone' Dodd

Arrangers include:
Clement 'Coxsone' Dodd, Richard Ace, Roland Alphonso, Denzil Laing, Robert 'Robbie' Lyn, Larry Marshall, Jackie Mittoo, Horace 'BB' Seaton & Leroy Sibbles

Engineers include:
Clement 'Coxsone' Dodd, Overton 'Scientist' Browne, Sid Bucknor, Hedley Jones, Larry Marshall, Sylvan Morris & Errol 'Errol T' Thompson

Labels: 1 Flash Hit, All Stars, Black Wax, Blue Mountain, Bongo Man, BRA (USA), Budget, Bugget, C and N, Cariboo, Collector's Series, Coxson, Coxsone, D Darling, Down Beat, Embassy, Faze Four, Festival '71, Festival '72, Forward, ICI Disc, Iron Side, London Records, Money Disc, Music City, Music Lab, Muzik City, ND Records, Port O Jam, Randycox (with Randy's Records), Remnant, Rolando & Powie, Scorpio, Sensational, Sight 'N' Sound, Sight & Sound (USA), Studio One, Super Natrual Disc (sic), Studio One, Super Six, Supreme, Tranquility (USA), Turn Table, Up Town, Wincox, (with Winston Chin Quee), Winro & Worldisc

Gospel Labels: Calvary Temple, Gospel, Refuge, Sacred, Tabernacle & The Fisherman

Affiliated Labels: Altone Disc (Alton Ellis), Antics Disc (Lord Antics), Big House (Horace Andy), Black Gold, Black Roots (Sugar Minott), Composer (Lord Composer), Date Disc (Lord Antics), Diamond (The Virtues/Rupie Edwards), Fatt (Jackie Mittoo), Forcox, Harry Jam (Sir Harry), Organaire (Charlie 'Organaire' Cameron), Konduko (Noel 'King Sporty' Williams), Lyn's (Robert 'Robbie' Lyn), Media Records (Lou Gooden), Tee Gee (Tony Gregory), Teen (Monty Alexander), Top Cat, Top Disc (Lou Gooden), Upsetter (Lee Perry) & Wail N Soul M (Bob Marley & The Wailing Wailers)

Musicians:
"Give thanks to all the numerous musicians who have shared in the different sessions…" **'I'm Flash Forward'**

Aubrey Adams & The Dew Droppers, Roland Alphonso & His Alley Cats, The Blues Blenders, The Brentford All Stars, The Brentford Boggie Band, The Brentford Disco Band, The Brentford Road All Stars, The Brentford Rockers, Karl Bryan & The Afrokats, Dodd & The Brentford Disco Set, The Caribbean Disco Band, The Coxsonairs, Don Drummond & The City Slickers, The Gladiators Band (Guitar: Albert Griffiths, Bass & Guitar: Clinton Fearon), Herman Hersang & His City Slickers, I'm & The Agg, The Liberation Group, The Mellow Cats, The Mighty Vikings, Jackie Mittoo & The Crusaders, Jackie Mittoo & The Pressure Boys, The Musle (sic) Souls, Count Ossie & The Cyclones, Monty & The Cyclones, The New Establishment, Ossie & The Upsetters, Lee Perry & The Dynamites, The Rhythm Aces, The Sheiks, Sir Coxson's All Stars, The Soul Boys, The Sound Defenders, The Studio One Orchestra & The Underground Vegetables

Clue J & His Blues Blasters
Drums: Arkland 'Drumbago' Parks & Ken Williams
Bass: Cluett 'Clue J' Johnson
Lead Guitar: Ernest Ranglin & Keith/Ian Stoddart
Rhythm Guitar: Ken Richards
Piano: Aubrey Adams & Monty Alexander
& Theophilus 'Easy Snappin'' Beckford
Tenor Saxophone: Roland Alphonso
Trombone: Emmanuel 'Rico' Rodriguez

The Skatalites

"The Skatalites consist of musicians who are the best individually and have combined to produce a sound that is the greatest."
    'Ska Authentic From Jamaica Volume Two'

Drums: Lloyd Knibb
Bass: Lloyd Brevett & Lloyd Spence
Guitar: Jerome 'Jah Jerry' Hines, Harold McKenzie, Ernest Ranglin & Nerlyn 'Lynn' Taitt
Piano: Gladstone Anderson & Jackie Mittoo
Organ & Harmonica: Charles 'Charlie Organaire' Cameron
Tenor Saxophone: Roland Alphonso & Tommy McCook
Alto Saxophone: Lester Sterling & Karl 'Cannonball' Bryan
Tenor & Baritone Saxophone: Dennis 'Ska' Campbell
Trumpet: Oswald 'Baba' Brooks, Reverend Billy Cooke, Percival Dillon, Bobby Ellis, Raymond Harper, David Madden & Johnny 'Dizzy' Moore
Trombone: Don Drummond & Ron 'Willow' Wilson
Vocals: Tony Da Costa, Dobby Dobson, Tony Gregory, Jackie Opel, Doreen Schaeffer & Lord Tamamo

The Soul Brothers
Drums: Joe Isaacs & Hector 'Bonnie'/'Bunny' Williams
Bass: Bryan Atkinson
Lead & Rhythm Guitar: Wallin Cameron & Harry Haughton
Piano & Organ: Jackie Mittoo
Tenor Saxophone: Roland Alphonso
Tenor & Baritone Saxophone: Dennis 'Ska' Campbell
Trumpet: Bobby Ellis

The Soul Vendors
Drums: Hector 'Bonnie'/'Bunny' Williams
Bass: Lloyd Brevett & Leroy Sibbles
Guitar: Ernest Ranglin, Nerlyn 'Lynn' Taitt & Errol Walters
Piano & Organ: Jackie Mittoo
Tenor Saxophone: Roland Alphonso
Alto Saxophone: Karl 'Cannonball' Bryan & Lester Sterling
Trumpet: Percival Dillon & Johnny 'Dizzy' Moore
Vocalists; Ken Boothe, Alton Ellis, Owen Gray & Peter Johnson

The Sound Dimension
Drums: Phil Callender, Joe Isaacs, Lloyd Knibb, Leroy 'Horse Mouth' Wallace & Hector 'Bonnie'/'Bunny' Williams
Bass: Boris Gardiner & Leroy Sibbles
Guitar: Eric 'Rickenbacker' Frater, Carlton Manning, Keith Scott & Ernest Ranglin
Piano & Organ: Aubrey Adams, Richard Ace, Robert 'Robbie' Lyn & Jackie Mittoo
Tenor Saxophone: Roland Alphonso, Felix 'Deadly' Hedley Bennett & Cedric 'I'm' Brooks
Alto Saxophone: Karl 'Cannonball' Bryan & Lester Sterling
Trumpet: David Madden
Trombone: Vincent 'Don D Junior' Gordon
Vibraphone: Lennie Hibbert
Percussion: Les 'Bongo Herman' Davis & Denzil Laing

The Soul Defenders
Drums: Louis Daley, Joseph Hill & Vin Morgan
Bass: Leroy Sibbles & Festus Walker
Guitar: Ronald Campbell, Eric 'Rickenbacker' Frater, 'Jah Privy', Frederick Thompson & Val Whittaker
Keyboards: Vin Morgan
Tenor Saxophone: Roland Alphonso
Percussion: Joseph Hill & Harry Powell

The Brentford Disco Set
Drums: Cleveland 'Clevie' Browne, Freddie McGregor & Leroy 'Horsemouth' Wallace
Bass: Earl 'Bagga' Walker
Guitar: Noel 'Sowell Radics' Bailey
Keyboards: Paul 'Pablove Black' Dixon, Jackie Mittoo & Bobby Kalphat
Tenor Saxophone: Glen Da Costa

Chapter 5

Studio One 13 Brentford Road Kingston 5th February 1991

Sources

Introduction
Interview with Winston 'Burning Spear' Rodney
London UK/New York USA 5th February 2001
Interviews with Bunny 'Striker' Lee London UK 23rd October 2007 & 17th October 2008
Interview with Roy Cousins London/Liverpool UK 3rd June 2016

Paul Coote, Noel Hawks, Dave Hendley & Chris Lane: Interview with Augustus Pablo
London UK 21st September 1996
Noel Hawks & Jah Floyd: Interviews with Bunny 'Striker' Lee
London UK 17th August 2006 & 6th December 2006

Steve Barrow & Peter Dalton: Reggae The Rough Guide Rough Guides Ltd 1997
Bill Bryson: Shakespeare William Collins 2016
Jim Godbolt: All This And Many A Dog Memoirs Of A Loser/Pessimist
Northway Publications 2007
Dave Hendley: Black Disciple An Interview With Winston Rodney The Burning Spear
Blues & Soul 239 & 240 October 1978
Tero Kaski: 'Clevie Browne' Mud Cannot Settle Without Water Muzik Tree/Black Star 1998
Chris Lane: Rad Bryan & Hux Brown *Blues & Soul* 125 December 1973/January 1974
Chris Lane: The Reggae Scene *Blues & Soul* 126 January 1974
Ian McCann: Bob Marley In His Own Words Omnibus Press 1993

Harry Hawke: Liner Notes for Red Bumb Ball Pressure Sounds PSCD/LP 40 2003
Harry Hawke: Liner Notes for Down Santic Way Pressure Sounds PSCD/LP 46 2005
Harry Hornby: Liner Notes for Flashing Echo Trojan In Dub 1970 to 1980
Trojan TJDDD051 2002

Liner Notes: Greatest Jamaican Beat Rock Steady Baba Boom Time
Treasure Isle LP 102/3 circa 1968

Roman Stewart: 'Hit Song' Arab 7" Produced by Tommy Cowan 1976
Dillinger: 'Natty Sings A Hit Song' Arab 7" Produced by Gayman Alberga 1976

Chapter 1 How It All Began
Motta's Recording Studio
Interview with Derrick Harriott London UK 22nd May 1998
Interview with Derrick Harriott London UK/Kingston Jamaica 20th June 1998
Interview with Brian Motta London UK/British Columbia Canada 13th April 2006
Interviews with Bunny 'Striker' Lee
London UK 23rd October 2007 & 17th September 2008

Noel Hawks & Jah Floyd: Interviews with Bunny 'Striker' Lee London UK
17th August 2006, 6th December 2006, 23rd October 2007, 21st October 2009
& 3rd October 2010
Laurence Cane-Honeysett: Interview with Graeme Goodall
London UK/Atlanta USA, January 2000

Sources

Steve Barrow & Peter Dalton: Reggae The Rough Guide Rough Guides 1997
Carl Gayle: 'This Is Reggae Music' *Black Music* Issue 28 Volume 3 March 1976
Ray Hitchins: Vibe Merchants The Sound Creators Of Jamaican Popular Music
Ashgate Publishing Limited 2014
David Katz: Solid Foundation An Oral History Of Reggae Bloomsbury Publishing Plc 2003
Earl Leaf: Isles Of Rhythm AS Barnes & Company 1948
Tom Murray (Editor & Arranger): Folk Songs Of Jamaica Oxford University Press 1951
Michael Turner & Robert Schoenfeld: Roots Knotty Roots Nighthawk Records 2001

Steve Barrow: Liner Notes Ernest Ranglin Below The Bassline Island
Jamaica Jazz IJCD 4002 1996
Paul Coote & Steve Barrow: Liner Notes Various Artists Mento Madness
(Motta's Jamaican Mento 1951 to 1956) V2 VVR1025512 2004
Richard Noblett: Liner Notes Various Artists Boogu Yagga Gal Jamaican Mento
Heritage HTCD45 2001

Liner Notes: Various Artists Independence Jump Up Calypso
Treasure Isle LP DR 1001 1 1966
Liner Notes: Various Artists Authentic Jamaican Calypsos (Volumes 1 to 5)
Motta's Recording Studio MOTL 101 to 105 1951 to 1956

Recommended Further Listening:
Various: Mento Madness Motta's Jamaican Mento 1951 to 1956 V2 VVR1025512 2004
Various: Take Me To Jamaica (The Story Of Jamaican Mento with Stanley Motta, Ivan Chin & Ken Khouri from 1951 to 1958) Pressure Sounds PSCD52 2006

Chapter 2 Mento Gets Another Mention
Chin's Radio Services & The Caribbean Recording Company Ltd
Interview with Ivan S Chin London UK/Toronto Canada 22nd April 2006
Interview with Don Gangadeen London/Newbury UK 29th April 2006
Interviews with Bunny 'Striker' Lee London UK 23rd October 2007 & 17th September 2008
Interview with Winston 'Merritone' Blake
London UK/New York USA 15th September 2011

Noel Hawks & Jah Floyd: Interviews with Bunny 'Striker' Lee London UK
17th August 2006, 6th December 2006, 23rd October 2007, 21st October 2009
& 3rd October 2010

Laurence Cane-Honeysett: Interview with Graeme Goodall
London UK/Atlanta USA January 2000
Paul Coote: Interview with Lloyd 'King Jammy' James Kingston Jamaica 9th August 1996
Hasse Huss: Interview with Uzziah 'Cool Stick' Thompson
Kingston Jamaica 26th October 1996

Mike Atherton: R&B in Jamaica 1947 to 1958 *Sailor's Delight* Number 11 1982
Steve Barrow & Peter Dalton: Reggae The Rough Guide, Rough Guides 1997
Ivan Chin: Recollections From Ivan Chin 2004 (revised February 2005)
Mark Gorney: 'Doctor Bird Graeme Goodall' *Full Watts* Volume 3 Number 3 May 1999

Peter Mason: 'Irving Burgie Obituary' *The Guardian* 6th December 2019
Tom Murray (Editor and Arranger): Folk Songs Of Jamaica, Oxford University Press 1951
Aaron Norman: 'The Belafonte Story' *Calypso* Number 1 1957
Kevin O'Brien Chang & Wayne Chen: Reggae Routes The Story of Jamaican Music
Ian Randle Publishers 1998
Michael Turner & Robert Schoenfeld: Roots Knotty Roots Nighthawk Records 2001
Martin Wong: 'Tough Gong Chinese Jamaican' *Giant Robot* Issue 37 Fall 2005

The Daily Gleaner Kingston Jamaica 11th February 1957

Belafonte Sings Chappell & Co Ltd 1962

Liner Notes: Authentic Jamaican Folk Songs featuring The Frats Quintet
Follow The Stars On Starline FLP 102 1962
Liner Notes: Carlos Malcolm & His Afro-Jamaican Rhythms (The Sound Of The Soil)
Space Flight UpBeat LP 102 1965
Liner Notes: Various Artists Meet Me In Jamaica (BWI) Authentic Calypsos
Monogram LP 12 852 circa 1959/1960
Liner Notes: Various Artists Authentic Jamaican Calypsos (Volumes 1 to 5)
Motta's Recording Studio MOTL 101 to 105 1951 to 1956

Recommended Further Listening:
Chin's Calypso Sextet: Chin's Calypso Sextet, Kingston Jamaica Volumes One to Five
Chin's CD Baby 2004/2005
Various: Take Me To Jamaica (The Story Of Jamaican Mento with Stanley Motta, Ivan Chin & Ken Khouri from 1951 to 1958) Pressure Sounds PSCD52 2006

Chapter 3 Sound Systems Were Like Our Radio Station
RJR & JBC
Interviews with Earl 'Little Roy' Lowe London UK 1st November 1995 & 22nd July 1999
Interview with Derrick Harriott London UK 22nd May 1998
Interview with Derrick Harriott London UK/Kingston Jamaica 20th June 1998
Interview with Winston 'Groovy' Tucker London UK 20th May 2004
Interviews with Leonard 'Santic' Chin London UK 29th December 2004, 29th October 2009 & 16th November 2009
Interview with Ivan S Chin London UK/Toronto Canada 22nd April 2006
Interviews with Bunny 'Striker' Lee London UK 23rd October 2007, 17th September 2008, 30th October 2012 & 9th November 2015
Interview with Pete Weston London UK/Kingston Jamaica 27th March 2008
Interview with Linval Thompson London UK/Kingston Jamaica 24th July 2008
Interview with Tony Rounce London UK 20th January 2009
Interview with Paul Khouri London UK/Kingston Jamaica 4th June 2009
Interview with Winston 'Merritone' Blake
London UK/New York USA 15th September 2011
Interview with Joseph 'Jo Jo' Hoo Kim
London UK/ New York USA 18th February 2014

Sources

Laurence Cane-Honeysett: Interview with Graeme Goodall
London UK/Atlanta USA January 2000
Paul Coote, Noel Hawks, Dave Hendley & Chris Lane:
Interview with Augustus Pablo London UK 21st September 1996
Paul Coote & Hasse Huss: Interview with Jimmy Radway St Mary Jamaica
4th December 1998
Noel Hawks & Jah Floyd: Interviews with Bunny 'Striker' Lee London UK 17th August 2006,
6th December 2006, 23rd October 2007, 21st October 2009, 3rd October 2010
& 30th October 2012
Noel Hawks, Jah Floyd & Diggory Kenrick: Interview with Dennis AlCapone
London UK 9th November 2015
Noel Hawks & Jah Floyd: Interview with Dennis AlCapone London UK 9th November 2015
Pete Holdsworth: Interviews with Joseph 'Jo Jo' Hookim
London UK/New York USA 4th September 1996 & 26th November 2000
Pete Holdsworth: Interview with Pete Weston
Tokyo Japan/Kingston Jamaica 25th March 2008
Pete Holdsworth: Interview with Jimmy Radway
Tokyo Japan/St Mary Jamaica 3rd September 2008
Hasse Huss: Interview with Uzziah 'Cool Stick' Thompson
Kingston Jamaica 26th October 1996
Naoki Ienaga: Interview with Ronnie Nasralla Florida USA April 2012
Chris Lane & Noel Hawks: Interview with Dave Barker London UK 5th December 2000

Mike Atherton: 'R&B in Jamaica 1947 to 1958' *Sailor's Delight* Number 11 1982
Stuart Baker: Studio One Rockers Special Edition Booklet Soul Jazz Records Ltd 2001
Steve Barrow & Peter Dalton: Reggae The Rough Guide Rough Guides 1997
Sebastian Clarke: Jah Music The Evolution Of The Popular Jamaican Song
Heinemann Educational Books Ltd 1980
Stephen Davis: Bob Marley The Biography Arthur Baker Limited 1983
Carl Gayle: 'Straight To The Nation's Head' *Black Music* Volume 3 Issue 26 January 1976
Carl Gayle: 'Marcus Garvey Meets The Rockers Uptown'
Black Music Volume 3 Issue 27 February 1976
Mark Gorney: 'Doctor Bird Graeme Goodall' *Full Watts* Volume 3 Number 2 May 1999
Mark Gorney: 'Doctor Bird Graeme Goodall'
Full Watts Volume 3 Number 3 Winter 1999/2000
Ray Hurford: 'Conscious Dread Mikey Dread' *Small Axe* Number 13 1984
Ray Hurford & Geoff Sullivan: 'Dennis AlCapone The First DJ Cup Winner'
More Axe Muzik Tree/Black Star 1984
Brian Jahn & Tom Weber: Reggae Island Jamaican Music In The Digital Age
Kingston Publishers Ltd 1992
Tero Kaski & Pekka Vuorinen: Reggae Inna Dance Hall Style Black Star 1984
David Katz: Solid Foundation An Oral History Of Reggae Bloomsbury Publishing Plc 2003
Chris Lane: 'Augustus 'Gussie' Clarke' 'The Reggae Scene' *Blues & Soul* 112
22nd June 1973
Chris Lane: 'The Reggae Scene' *Blues & Soul* 130 12th March 1974
Chris Lane: 'Big Youth Revisited' 'The Reggae Scene' *Blues & Soul* 134 7th May 1974
Chris Lane: 'Prince Buster' 'Skanking' *Blues & Soul* 140 30th July 1974
Chris Lane: 'The Big Youth Story' *Pressure Drop* Issue Two 1977
Keeble McFarlane: 'Canada's Early Contribution To Local Broadcasting'

Jamaica Observer 22nd January 2011
Chris May: 'Ever Changing Stylee' *Black Music & Jazz Review*
Volume 3 Issue 11 March 1981
Steve Milne: 'Mikey Dread Come Fe Conquer' *Full Watts* Volume 3 Number 2 May 1999
Kevin O'Brien Chang & Wayne Chen: Reggae Routes The Story of Jamaican Music
Ian Randle Publishers 1998
Basil Walters: Galbraith 'The Radio Man And Sound System Innovator'
Jamaica Observer 6th June 2010
Timothy White: Catch a Fire The Definitive Edition Omnibus Press 2006
Various: The Guinness Who's Who Of Reggae Square One/Guinness Publishing 1994
Merry Go Round *The Daily Gleaner* Kingston Jamaica 31st October 1969

Steve Barrow: Liner Notes Ska Down Jamaica Way Top Deck LP TDLP101 1995
Dr. Buster Dynamite: Liner Notes It's Shuffle 'N' Ska Time with Lloyd 'The Matador' Daley
Jamaican Gold JMC 200 216 1994
Paul Coote: Liner Notes Keep The Pressure Down Fe Me Time CD/LP FMT01 1999
Dave Katz & Chris Wilson: Liner Notes Lee 'Scratch' Perry & The Upsetters
The Upsetter Shop 2 1969 to 1973 Heartbeat 7601 1999

Liner Notes: Meet Me In Jamaica (BWI) Authentic Calypsos
Monogram LP 12 852 circa 1959

History Of Radio Jamaica Ltd Dub Foundation Irie FM (Jamaica) 3rd July 1994

The Melodians: 'Swing And Dine' High Note 7" produced by Sonia Pottinger 1968
Ray I: 'Weatherman Skank' Black & White 7" produced by Carlton Patterson 1979

Chapter 4 Federal Country... Another Hit!
Records Ltd & Federal Records
Interviews with Roy Cousins London/Liverpool UK 27th April 2002 & 3rd June 2016
Interview with Derrick Morgan London UK/Kingston Jamaica 17th July 2003
Interview with Brian Motta London UK/British Columbia Canada 13th April 2006
Interviews with Bunny 'Striker' Lee London UK 23rd October 2007, 17th October 2008
& 17th September 2008
Interview with Paul Khouri London UK/Kingston Jamaica 4th June 2009
Interview with Winston 'Merritone' Blake London UK/New York USA 15th September 2011
Interview with Roy Cousins Liverpool UK 24th March 2014
Interview with Ronnie Nasralla London UK/Atlanta USA 30th September 2014
Interview with Keith 'Scotty' Scott London UK/Los Angeles USA 23rd May 2019

Laurence Cane-Honeysett: Interview with Graeme Goodall
London UK/Atlanta USA January 2000
Noel Hawks & Jah Floyd: Interviews with Bunny 'Striker' Lee London UK 17th August 2006
& 6th December 2006
Naoki Ienaga: Interview with Paul Khouri Kingston Jamaica 13th July 2004

Sources

Mike Atherton: 'R&B In Jamaica 1947 to 1958' *Sailor's Delight* Number 11 1982
Steve Barrow & Peter Dalton: Reggae The Rough Guide Rough Guides Limited 1997
Sebastian Clarke: Jah Music The Evolution Of The Popular Jamaican Song Heinemann Educational Books 1980
Roy Cousins: The Royals 'The Climate Always Hot' Spring 2002
Roger Dalke: More Scorcha From Studio One TSI Publications 1997
Carl Gayle: 'This Is Reggae Music' *Black Music* Volume 3 Issue 28 March 1976
Mark Gorney: 'Doctor Bird Graeme Goodall' *Full Watts* Volume 3 Number 2 May 1999
Mark Gorney: 'Doctor Bird Graeme Goodall' *Full Watts* Volume 3 Number 3 Winter 1999/2000
Noel Hawks & Jah Floyd: Reggae Going International 1967 to 1976 The Bunny 'Striker' Lee Story Jamaican Recordings Publishing 2012
Ray Hitchins: Vibe Merchants The Sound Creators Of Jamaican Popular Music Ashgate Publishing Limited 2014
David Katz: Solid Foundation An Oral History Of Reggae Bloomsbury Publishing Plc 2003
Chris Lane: 'Mikey Boo' 'The Reggae Scene' *Blues & Soul* 124 7th December 1973
Chris Lane: 'The Reggae Scene' *Blues & Soul* 126 15th January 1974
Kevin O'Brien Chang & Wayne Chen: Reggae Routes The Story of Jamaican Music Ian Randle Publishers 1998
David Roberts (Managing Editor): British Hit Singles & Albums Guinness World Records Limited 2005
Robert Schoenfeld: 'Interview with Lynn Taitt' *Dub Catcher* Volume 1 Issue 4 June 1992
Michael Turner & Robert Schoenfeld: Roots Knotty Roots Nighthawk Records 2001
Michael E Veal: Dub Soundscapes & Shattered Songs In Jamaican Reggae Wesleyan University Press 2007

AW: 'Calypso Singers 'Sell' Jamaica' *The Daily Gleaner* Kingston Jamaica 19th June 1954
'Gramophone Records To Be Made Here'
The Daily Gleaner Kingston Jamaica 17th September 1954

Liner Notes: Authentic Jamaican Folk Songs featuring The Frats Quintet Follow The Stars On Starline FLP 102 1962
Liner Notes: Carlos Malcolm & His Afro-Jamaican Rhythms (The Sound Of The Soil) Space Flight UpBeat LP 102 1965
Liner Notes: Byron Lee & The Dragonaires Plays Jamaica Ska Kentone Records LP107 circa 1964
Liner Notes: Rock Steady Greatest Hits Lynn Taitt & The Jets Merritone LP 205 circa 1967

Chapter 5 Dancing To The Music Of Sir Coxsone The Downbeat Studio One
Interview with Winston 'Burning Spear' Rodney London UK/New York USA 5th February 2001
Interview with Earl Sixteen London UK 8th January 2003
Interviews with Roy Cousins London/Liverpool UK 27th April 2002, 6th & 13th July 2004, 5th November 2008 & 3rd June 2016
Interviews with Bunny 'Striker' Lee London UK 23rd October 2007 & 17th September 2008
Interviews with Leonard 'Santic' Chin London UK 29th October & 16th November 2009
Interview with Roy Cousins Liverpool UK 24th March 2014
Interview with Horace Andy London UK/Kingston Jamaica 23rd October 2015
Interview with Owen Gray London/Bilston UK 25th October 2019

Sources

Paul Coote, Noel Hawks, Dave Hendley & Chris Lane: Interview with Augustus Pablo London UK 21st September 1996
Paul Coote & Hasse Huss: Interview with Jimmy Radway St Mary Jamaica 4th December 1998
Chris Lane & Noel Hawks: Interview with Dave Barker London UK 5th December 2000
Jah Floyd & Noel Hawks: Interviews with Bunny 'Striker' Lee London UK 17th August & 6th December 2006
Jah Floyd & Noel Hawks: Interview with Dennis AlCapone London UK 9th November 2015

Heather Augustyn & Adam Reeves: Alpha Boys' School Cradle Of Jamaican Music Half Pint Press 2017
Steve Barrow: Clement 'Sir Coxsone' Dodd And The Rise Of Studio One Records The Album Cover Art Of Studio One Records Soul Jazz Books 2011
Steve Barrow & Peter Dalton: Reggae The Rough Guide Rough Guides Ltd 1997
Laurence Cane Honeysett: 'Earl Morgan' *Full Watts* Volume 3 Number 3 Winter 1999
Rob Chapman: Downbeat Special Studio One Album Discography 1985 Updated 1996
Rob Chapman: Never Grow Old Studio One Singles Listing & Rhythm Directory 1989 Updated 1992, 1994 & 1999
Sebastian Clarke: Jah Music (The Evolution Of The Popular Jamaican Song) Heinemann Educational Books 1980
Roy Cousins: 'The Royals 'The Climate Always Hot'' Spring 2002
Roger Dalke: A Scorcha From Studio One TSI Publications 1997
Roger Dalke: More Scorcha From Studio One TSI Publications 1997
Roger Dalke: The House Of Bamboo Top Sounds International Publications 1985
Jim Dooley: 'Bagga' *Full Watts* Volume 5 Number 2 Spring 2004
Ray Hurford: 'Top One Hundred Rhythms 1984 to 1985' *Small Axe* Number 26 1988
Howard Johnson & Jim Pines: Reggae Deep Roots Music, Proteus Books 1982
Tero Kaski: 'Clevie Browne' Mud Cannot Settle Without Water Muzik Tree/Black Star 1998
Tero Kaski: 'Sylvan Morris Tales Of Brentford Road' More Axe 7 Muzik Tree/Black Star 1989
David Katz: Solid Foundation An Oral History Of Reggae, Bloomsbury Publishing Plc 2003
David Katz: 'Clement 'Sir Coxsone' Dodd Obituary' *The Guardian* 6th May 2004
David Katz: 'One Step Beyond' *Mojo* Issue 136 March 2005
Beth & Dave Kingston: 'Hedley Jones' Mud Cannot Settle Without Water Muzik Tree/Black Star 1998
Chris Lane: 'The Reggae Scene' 'Junior Lincoln' *Blues & Soul* 118 14th September 1973
Chris Lane: 'Skanking' 'All The Way From Brentford Road' *Blues & Soul* 171 14th October 1975
Chris Lane: 'Tribute To Studio One' *Pressure Drop* Issue Two 1976
Chris Lane: 'Studio One The Essential Dubs' *Black Music* Volume 2 Issue 11 March 1980
James Maycock: 'Still Massive After All These Years' *The Independent* 19th June 1998
Claude Mills: 'Sir Coxsone Dodd The Dark Knight Of Jamaican Music' *The Sunday Gleaner* 13th April 1997
Steve Milne: 'Alton Ellis Forty Years Of Musical Excellence' *Full Watts* Volume 3 Number 3 Winter 1999
Steve Milne: 'First Lady Marcia Griffiths' *Full Watts* Volume 4 Number 1 Spring 2000
Dorothy E. Mittoo-Walker: The Magical Fountain Of Love (In Memory Of Jackie Mittoo) Dare Books 1994
Ian McCann: 'Dennis Brown Life Goes In Circles' More Axe 7 Muzik Tree/Black Star 1989

Charlie Morgan: Coxson's Music Outernational Records 1997
Kevin O'Brien Chang & Wayne Chen: Reggae Routes The Story Of Jamaican Music
Ian Randle Publishers 1998
John Public & Miss Pat: 'BB Seaton' *Full Watts* Volume 5 Number 4 Spring 2004
Michael Turner & Robert Schoenfeld: Roots Knotty Roots Nighthawk Records 2001
Michael E Veal: Dub Soundscapes & Shattered Songs In Jamaican Reggae
Wesleyan University Press 2007
Trevor Williams & Rich Lowe: Coxsone Dodd & Studio One
Reggae Directory Volume 4 Number 2 1992

'Norma Dodd Dies' *The Gleaner* 2nd September 2010

Stuart Baker: Liner Notes Interview With Mr CS Dodd
Studio One Rockers Special Edition Booklet Soul Jazz SJR CD 48 2001
CS Dodd: Liner Notes Oldies But Goodies Volume One Studio One LP GW 0002 circa 1968
Louis N Gooden: Liner Notes In Memory Of Don Drummond Studio One LP 1969
Harry Hawke: Liner Notes The Heptones Peace And Harmony The Trojan Anthology 1966 to 1979 Trojan CDTJDDD 202 2004
Harry Hawke: Liner Notes Earl Sixteen Soldier Of Jah Army 1976 to 1982
Patate Records PRP 014 2003
Noel Hawks: Liner Notes Burning Spear Sounds From The Burning Spear
Soul Jazz SJR LP/CD 101 2003
Noel Hawks: Liner Notes Coxsone's Music 2 Soul Jazz SJR LP/CD 332 2016

Liner Notes: Cedric 'I'm' Brooks I'm Flash Forward Studio One LP 1977
Liner Notes: Dub Specialist Juk's Incorporation Parts One & Two Studio One LP circa 1977
Liner Notes: Freddie McGregor Bobby Bobylon Studio One LP 1980
Liner Notes: Jackie Mittoo Evening Time Coxsone CSL 8012 circa 1968
Liner Notes: Various Mama Peckings And The Dutchess
Peckings Treasure Isle LP PTI 001 2004
Liner Notes: Various Ska Authentic From Jamaica Volume Two Studio One LP circa 1964
Liner Notes: Various Soul Vendors On Tour Coxsone CSL 8010 1967

Owen Gray: 'On The Beach' Cariboo 7" produced by Clement 'Coxsone' Dodd 1960
Owen Gray: 'On The Beach' Dice 7" 45/CC3 (UK) produced by Clement 'Coxsone' Dodd 1962
Sound Dimension: 'More Scorchia' Coxsone 7" produced by Clement 'Coxsone' Dodd 1968

Recommended Further Reading:
Stuart Baker & Steve Barrow: The Album Cover Art Of Studio One Records
Soul Jazz Books 2011
Rob Chapman: Downbeat Special Studio One Album Discography 1985
Updated 1996
Rob Chapman: Never Grow Old Studio One Singles Listing & Rhythm Directory 1989
Updated 1992, 1994, 1999 & 2016
Roger Dalke: A Scorcha From Studio One TSI Publications 1997
Roger Dalke: More Scorcha From Studio One TSI Publications 1997
Charlie Morgan: Coxson's Music Outernational Records 1997

Acknowledgements

I'm sure that most people wince when they see the list on CD and book credits running from the lady who makes the tea all the way up to The Almighty but it has to be said that these projects, and this one in particular, would have proved completely impossible without the help and guidance of all of the following and many more. I know how annoying and upsetting, both personally and professionally, it can be when you have given someone a lot of help and you don't even get a credit. So extra special thanks to:

Dennis AlCapone, Horace Andy, Mike Atherton, Stuart Baker, Dave Barker, Steve Barker, Steve Barrow, Winston 'Merritone' Blake (RIP), Laurence Cane-Honeysett, Rob Chapman, Clive Chin, Ivan S Chin (RIP), Leonard 'Santic' Chin (RIP), Herman Chin-Loy, Augustus 'Gussie' Clarke, Paul Coote, David Corio, Roy Cousins, Tommy Cowan, Roger Dalke, Peter Dalton, Michael De Koningh (RIP), Carl 'Captain Sinbad' Dwyer, Vince Ellis, Dave Feneron, Don Gangadeen, Carl Gayle, Graeme Goodall (RIP), Mark Gorney, Owen Gray, Lars Gredal, Gary Hall, Derrick Harriott, Dave Hendley (RIP), Pete Holdsworth, Clive Holloway, Joseph 'Jo Jo' Hoo Kim (RIP), Ray Hurford, Hasse Huss, Naoki Ienaga, Lloyd 'King Jammy' James, Penny Jones (RIP), Tero Kaski (RIP) & Seija Kouva, David Katz, Dave Kingston, Chris Lane, Bunny 'Striker' Lee OD, Pat & Ian Lacey, Beth Lesser/Kingston, Earl 'Little Roy' Lowe, Frank Malone, Ian McCann, Steve Milne, Brian Motta, Ronnie Nasralla, Andrew Neale, Chris O'Brien, Augustus Pablo (RIP), Jimmy Radway, Pete Reilly, David Rodigan MBE, Winston 'Burning Spear' Rodney, Tony Rounce, Keith 'Scotty' Scott, Karl Shale, Jim Silles, Dana Smart, Aaron 'English' Smith, Karen Tate, Ossie 'Black Solidarity' Thomas, Linval Thompson, Uzziah 'Cool Stick' Thompson (RIP), Winston 'Groovy' Tucker, Pekka Vuorinen, Pete Weston, Olston Wiltshire and many, many more…

All were generous, patient and gracious but legendary producer Bunny 'Striker' Lee and singer/producer extraordinaire Roy Cousins of The Royals were both particularly unstinting in their co-operation and support and deserve special thanks

Thank you to Aaron 'English' Smith, Carl 'Captain Sinbad' Dwyer & Ossie 'Black Solidarity' Thomas (& his brothers Howie & Chris) for showing me how things run in Kingston, Jamaica

Without Brian Motta's patience, insight and powers of recall the opening chapter could never have been written

Without Ivan Chin's patience, insight and powers of recall the second chapter could never have been written

Without Laurence Cane-Honeysett's generosity the third and fourth chapters could never have been written

Without Paul Khouri's patience, insight and powers of recall and Naoki Ienaga's generosity the fourth chapter could never have been written

My grateful and sincere thanks to Steve Barrow, Laurence Cane-Honeysett, Paul Coote, Dave Hendley RIP, Ray Hurford, David Katz, Seija Kouva (for Tero Kaski RIP), Chris Lane, Beth Lesser/Kingston & Steve Milne for their kind permission in allowing me to quote from their works and to Steve Barrow, Maria Green, Chris Lane, Ian McCann & Tony Rounce for generously reviewing the manuscript, for their attention to detail and for sharing their in depth knowledge. Any errors that remain are mine alone...

With grateful thanks, sincere gratitude and love to Anna, Maria & Manny for their endless patience and unfailing support

My sincere apologies to anyone whose name I have inadvertently omitted

About the authors

Noel Hawks
Noel 'Harry Hawke' Hawks is the author, with Jah Floyd, of 'Reggae Going International 1967-1976 The Bunny Striker Lee Story', 'Songs Of Freedom: Complete Lyrics of Bob Marley', co-author, with Ian McCann, of the 2004 edition of 'The Complete Guide To The Music Of Bob Marley', co-author with Stuart Baker & Steve Barrow of 'Reggae 45 Sound System The Label Art Of Reggae Singles' and helped to compile 'The Guinness Who's Who Of Reggae'. He has also contributed to 'Covers: Retracing Reggae Record Sleeves In London' by Alex Bartsch, 'Clarks In Jamaica' by Al Fingers, 'Reggae Deep Roots Music' by Howard Johnson & Jim Pines, 'Skinhead' by Nick Knight and 'The Story Of Trojan Records' by Laurence Cane-Honeysett.

Noel has written for Billboard, Music Week, Record Collector, Vox, The Wire and numerous other magazines and has compiled and written sleeve notes for over 300 reggae releases on Bear Family, Blood & Fire, Burning Sounds, Dub Store, Fashion, Greensleeves, Jamaican Recordings, Pressure Sounds, Secret, Soul Jazz, Trojan, Universal and VP.

Jah Floyd
Jah Floyd has compiled and released over 150 reggae re-releases for the Jamaican Recordings and Kingston Sounds labels.

Also available:

**Reggae Going International
1967 to 1976
The Bunny 'Striker' Lee Story
Noel Hawks & Jah Floyd
Jamaican Recordings Publishing**

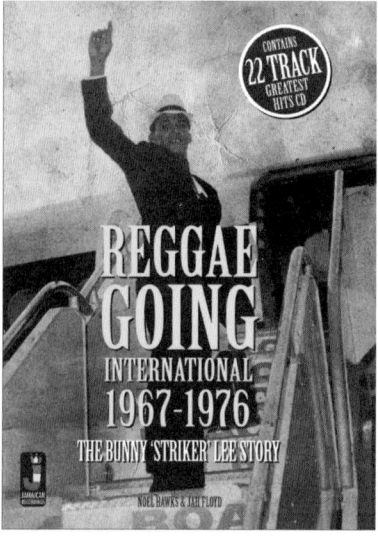

"In a career that has lasted for over forty years Bunny 'Striker' Lee has faithfully met the needs of his audience for music that accurately reflected their concerns and, in the process, enjoyed huge hits and provided work for dozens of singers, musicians and studio technicians. His contribution to the story of Jamaican music has been as great, if not greater, than that of many, more celebrated, men."
Steve Barrow,
Co-author of 'Reggae The Rough Guide'

In 2008 the Jamaican Government conferred the Order of Distinction on Bunny 'Striker' Lee for more than forty years of dedicated service to the music industry. Here, in Striker's own words, is the incredible story of how reggae went international…

Nominated for the 2012 Association for Recorded Sound Collections Awards for Excellence in Historical Recorded Sound Research

"Quite simply an incredibly important historical document"
David Rodigan MBE

"Here's the history of Jamaican music told in an utterly authentic way through the words of one man"
Ian McCann
Record Collector

2012 Pop Music Books of the Year
Independent on Sunday

*****Mojo
*****Record Collector
*****Riddim

I AM THE GORGON
BUNNY 'STRIKER' LEE & THE ROOTS OF REGGAE

Directed by musician and film maker, Diggory Kenrick, and narrated by legendary deejay, Dennis AlCapone, this acclaimed documentary tells the larger than life tale of legendary record producer, Bunny 'Striker' Lee charting his rise from motorcycle mechanic and record plugger to reggae's most successful record producer in the Seventies. Striker's story involves politics, arguments, gangs and guns as Jamaican music moved from ska to rock steady, from dub to dancehall, from the ghettos of Kingston to the world stage.

Featuring an amazing roll call including:
Singers: Horace Andy, Ken Boothe, Cornell Campbell, Johnny Clarke, Stranger Cole, Errol Dunkley, Winston Francis, John Holt, Derrick Morgan, Jimmy Riley, Max Romeo, BB Seaton, Roy Shirley & Linval Thompson

Vocal Groups: The Blackstones & The Twinkle Brothers

Deejays: Dennis AlCapone, Dr Alimantado, Dillinger, Prince Jazzbo, Jah Stitch, Trinity, U Roy & Tapper Zukie

Musicians: Aston 'Family Man' Barrett, Carlton 'Santa' Davis, Sly Dunbar, Robbie Shakespeare & Earl 'Chinna' Smith

Record Producers: King Jammy, Niney The Observer, Lee 'Scratch' Perry & Scientist
And many, many more…

Coming soon...

Jamaican Recordings
A History Of The Jamaican Recording Industry Part Two
Rock Steady To Rockers: From Treasure Isle To Channel One
Treasure Isle, Dynamic Sounds, Randy's Studio 17, Harry J, Joe Gibbs, King Tubby & Channel One

Jamaican Recordings
A History Of The Jamaican Recording Industry Part Three
The Upsetter To The Computer: From The Black Ark To Firehouse
The Black Ark, Aquarius, Tuff Gong, King Jammy, King Tubby In The Digital Age & A Brief History of Dub

Kingston Sounds Catalogue

Kingston Sounds Catalogue

CAT No: KSCD001/KSLP001

CAT No: KSCD007/KSLP007

CAT No: KSCD013/KSLP013

CAT No: KSCD019/KSLP019

CAT No: KSCD025/KSLP025

CAT No: KSCD031/KSLP031

CAT No: KSCD037/KSLP037

CAT No KSCD002/KSLP 002

CAT No: KSCD008/KSLP008

CAT No: KSCD014/KSLP013

CAT No: KSCD020/KSLP020

CAT No: KSCD026/KSLP026

CAT No KSCD032/KSLP032

CAT No KSCD038/KSLP038

CAT No KSCD003/KSLP003

CAT No CD: KSCD009/KSLP009

CAT No: KSCD015/KSLP015

CAT No: KSCD021/KSLP021

CAT No: KSCD027/KSLP027

CAT No: KSCD033/KSLP033

CAT No KSCD039/KSLP039

CAT No KSCD004/KSLP004

CAT No: KSCD010/KSLP010

CAT No: KSCD016/KSLP016

CAT No: KSCD022/KSLP022

CAT No: KSCD028/KSLP028

CAT No: KSCD034/KSLP034

CAT No: KSCD040/KSLP040

CAT No KSCD005/KSLP005

CAT No CD: KSCD011/KSLP011

CAT No: KSCD017/KSLP017

CAT No: KSCD 023 / KSLP 023

CAT No: KSCD029/KSLP029

CAT No KSCD 035/KSLP035

CAT No KSCD041/KSLP041

CAT No: KSCD006/KSLP006

CAT No KSCD012/KSLP012

CAT No: KSCD018/KSLP018

CAT No: KSCD024/KSLP024

CAT No: KSCD030/KSLP 030

CAT No: KSCD036/KSLP 036

CAT No: KSCD042/KSLP042

Kingston Sounds Catalogue

 CAT No: KSCD043/KSLP043
 CAT No: KSCD049/KSLP049
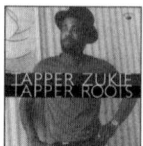 CAT No: KSCD055/KSLP055
 CAT No: KSCD061/KSLP061
 CAT No: KSCD067/KSLP067
 CAT No: KSCD073/KSLP073

 CAT No: KSCD044/KSLP044
 CAT No: KSCD050/KSLP050
 CAT No: KSCD056/KSLP056
 CAT No: KSCD062/KSLP062
 CAT No: KSCD068/KSLP068
 CAT No: KSCD074/KSLP074

 CAT No CD: KSCD045/KSLP045
 CAT No: KSCD051/KSLP051
 CAT No: KSCD057/KSLP057
 CAT No: KSCD063/KSLP063
 CAT No: KSCD069/KSLP069
 CAT No: KSCD075/KSLP075

 CAT No: KSCD046/KSLP046
 CAT No: KSCD052/KSLP052
 CAT No: KSCD058/KSLP058
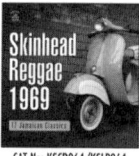 CAT No: KSCD064/KSLP064
 CAT No: KSCD070/KSLP070
 CAT No: KSCD076/KSLP076

 CAT No CD: KSCD047/KSLP047
 CAT No: KSCD053/KSLP053
 CAT No: KSCD059/KSLP059
 CAT No: KSCD065/KSLP065
 CAT No: KSCD071/KSLP071
 CAT No: KSCD077/KSLP077

 CAT No KSCD048/KSLP048
 CAT No: KSCD054/KSLP054
 CAT No: KSCD060/KSLP060
 CAT No: KSCD066/KSLP 066
 CAT No: KSCD072/KSLP072
 CAT No: KSCD078/KSLP078

Jamaican Recordings Catalogue

CAT No: JRCD001/JRLP001

CAT No: JRCD007/JRLP007

CAT No: JRCD013/JRLP013

CAT No: JRCD019/JRLP019

CAT No: JRCD025/JRLP025

CAT No: JRCD031/JRLP031

CAT No: JRCD002/JRLP002

CAT No: JRCD008/JRLP008

CAT No: JRCD014/JRLP014

CAT No: JRCD020/JRLP020

CAT No: JRCD026/JRLP026

CAT No: JRCD032/JRLP032

CAT No: JRCD003/JRLP003

CAT No: JRCD009/JRLP009

CAT No: JRCD015/JRLP015

CAT No: JRCD021/JRLP021

CAT No: JRCD027/JRLP027

CAT No: JRCD033/JRLP033

CAT No: JRCD004/JRLP004

CAT No: JRCD010/JRLP0010

CAT No: JRCD016/JRLP0016

CAT No: JRCD022/JRLP022

CAT No: JRCD028/JRLP028

CAT No: JRCD034/JRLP034

CAT No: JRCD005/JRLP005

CAT No: JRCD 0011/JRLP0011

CAT No: JRCD017/JRLP0017

CAT No: JRCD023/JRLP023

CAT No: JRCD029/JRLP029

CAT No: JRCD035/JRLP035

CAT No: JRCD 006/JRLP006

CAT No: JRCD012/JRLP0012

CAT No: JRCD018/JRLP0018

CAT No: JRCD024/JRLP024

CAT No: JRCD030/JRLP030

CAT No: JRCD036/JRLP036

 CAT No: JRCD037/JRLP037
 CAT No: JRCD043/JRLP043
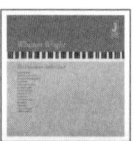 CAT No: JRCD049/JRLP049
 CAT No: JRCD055/JRLP055
 CAT No: JRCD061/JRLP061
 CAT No: JRCD067/JRLP067

 CAT No: JRCD038/JRLP038
 CAT No: JRCD044/JRLP044
 CAT No: JRCD050/JRLP050
 CAT No: JRCD056/JRLP056
 CAT No: JRCD062/JRLP062
 CAT No: JRCD068/JRLP068

 CAT No: JRCD039/JRLP039
 CAT No: JRCD045/JRLP045
 CAT No: JRCD051/JRLP051
 CAT No: JRCD057/JRLP057
 CAT No: JRCD063/JRLP063
 CAT No: JRCD069/JRLP069

 CAT No: JRCD040/JRLP040
 CAT No: JRCD046/JRLP046
 CAT No: JRCD052/JRLP052
 CAT No: JRCD058/JRLP058
 CAT No: JRCD064/JRLP064
 CAT No: JRCD070/JRLP070

 CAT No: JRCD041/JRLP041
 CAT No: JRCD047/JRLP047
 CAT No: JRCD053/JRLP053
 CAT No: JRCD059/JRLP059
 CAT No: JRCD065/JRLP065
 CAT No: JRCD071/JRLP071

 CAT No: JRCD042/JRLP042
 CAT No: JRCD048/JRLP048
 CAT No: JRCD054/JRLP054
 CAT No: JRCD060/JRLP060
 CAT No: JRCD066/JRLP066
 CAT No: JRCD072/JRLP072